CITYSPOTS
KRAK

WHAT'S IN YOUR GUIDEBOOK?

Independent authors Impartial up-to-date information from our travel experts who meticulously source local knowledge.

Experience Thomas Cook's 165 years in the travel industry and guidebook publishing enriches every word with expertise you can trust.

Travel know-how Thomas Cook has thousands of staff working around the globe, all living and breathing travel.

Editors Travel-publishing professionals, pulling everything together to craft a perfect blend of words, pictures, maps and design.

You, the traveller We deliver a practical, no-nonsense approach to information, geared to how you really use it.

ABOUT THE AUTHOR

Based in Lithuania and the Balkans, Richard 'Sco' Schofield has been writing about and taking photographs of the more exotic parts of Europe for almost a decade. Having started his travel-writing career in Cuba, Sco now runs a travel-publishing business with two colleagues in Tirana and is a regular contributor at the European city guide publisher, In Your Pocket. Most recently, he co-authored the *Thomas Cook Travellers Guide to Albania*.

CITYSPOTS
KRAKOW

Richard Schofield

Written & updated by Richard Schofield

Published by Thomas Cook Publishing
A division of Thomas Cook Tour Operations Limited
Company registration No: 3772199 England
The Thomas Cook Business Park, 9 Coningsby Road
Peterborough PE3 8SB, United Kingdom
Email: books@thomascook.com, Tel: +44 (0)1733 416477
www.thomascookpublishing.com

Produced by The Content Works Ltd
Aston Court, Kingsmead Business Park, Frederick Place
High Wycombe, Bucks HP11 1LA
www.thecontentworks.com

Series design based on an original concept by Studio 183 Limited

ISBN: 978-1-84848-136-7

First edition © 2007 Thomas Cook Publishing
This second edition © 2009 Thomas Cook Publishing
Text © Thomas Cook Publishing
Maps © Thomas Cook Publishing/PCGraphics (UK) Limited
Transport map © Communicarta Limited

Series Editor: Lucy Armstrong
Production/DTP: Steven Collins

Printed and bound in Spain by GraphyCems

Cover photography ((The gilded roof of Wawel Cathedral's Sigismund Chapel)
© David Robertson/Alamy

CONTENTS

INTRODUCING KRAKOW

Introduction....................8
When to go 10
Jewish Festival of Culture.....14
History..........................16
Lifestyle........................18
Culture..........................20

MAKING THE MOST OF KRAKOW

Shopping........................24
Eating & drinking 27
Entertainment
&nightlife........................31
Sport & relaxation 34
Accommodation 37
The best of Krakow...............42
Suggested itineraries 44
Something for nothing........46
When it rains 48
On arrival......................50

THE CITY OF KRAKOW

The old town & Wawel........60
Kazimierz 78
Further afield 90

OUT OF TOWN TRIPS

Nowa Huta 104
Zakopane 116

PRACTICAL INFORMATION

Directory.........................128
Emergencies 138

INDEX 140

MAPS

Krakow 52
Krakow transport map........56
The old town & Wawel........62
Kazimierz 80
Further afield 92
Krakow region 106

SYMBOLS KEY

The following symbols are used throughout this book:

ⓐ address ⓣ telephone ⓦ website address ⓛ opening times
ⓝ public transport connections ⓘ important

The following symbols are used on the maps:

🛈	information office	◼	points of interest
✈	airport	O	city
➕	hospital	O	large town
🛡	police station	○	small town
🚍	bus station	=	motorway
🚆	railway station	—	main road
✝	cathedral	—	minor road
❶	numbers denote featured	—	railway
	cafés & restaurants		

Hotels and restaurants are graded by approximate price as follows:
£ budget price ££ mid-range price £££ expensive

▶ St Andrew's Church, one of the oldest in Krakow

Introduction

Poland's splendid former capital, Krakow is the country's
number one tourist attraction. A UNESCO-protected old town,
extraordinary Jewish heritage and a complicated and often
bloody past all add up to make the ancient seat of Polish kings
and queens a destination that warrants further investigation.
A magnet whose force has drawn in such diverse historical
characters as invading Mongol hordes, Lenin and the late Pope
John Paul II over the centuries, Krakow offers an irresistible
blend of old and new sights and sensations to anyone with the
airfare and time to see it.

   With just three-quarters of a million inhabitants, Krakow
lacks the irritating bustle of the country's delirious capital to
the north. An almost provincial feel gives the city a charm that
pulls many an unsuspecting tourist into its clutches, making
expats out of people who long ago visited for the weekend and
who now find themselves married to the girl or boy they met
in a bar half a decade ago. But don't let the rustic image fool
you. Complete with vast shopping malls and more cutting edge
clubs than you could visit in a month, Krakow is also a modern
city, and it's perhaps this heady mix of styles that makes it one
of the best destinations in Eastern Europe.

   Krakow also enjoys the happy accident of finding itself in the
middle of the country's number-one tourist region. When you've
exhausted the sights and sensations in the city centre, there's
still plenty more to discover not too far away. From the unique
socialist realist sights of nearby Nowa Huta to the numerous
attractions on offer in Poland's winter capital, Zakopane, Krakow

is an ideal springboard for prolonged visits that will continue to remain affordable for the next decade at least. With its biscuit-tin architecture, catwalk females and heart-wrenching history, Krakow is a city that demands to be seen.

⬤ Krakow is a compelling mix of ancient and modern

When to go

SEASONS & CLIMATE

A country of extremes, 1963 saw winter temperatures in Krakow plummet to −35°C, while a few months later the population were flopping about in temperatures of +40°C. This is the magic of Poland. Whereas Western Europe witnesses year-round temperatures that barely nudge the mercury, Poland can boast real seasons. With the exception of the usual unexpected downpours, Krakow enjoys hot and sunny summers and the kind of winters that'll keep scarf-makers in business for centuries.

ANNUAL EVENTS

The official events website is at ⓦ www.biurofestiwalowe.pl. The same people publish an excellent bilingual monthly magazine, *Karnet*, full of information about events, concerts and exhibitions throughout the city. Another excellent source of information in English can be found online at ⓦ www.cracowonline.com

January
Wieliczka Salt Mines Concert The annual New Year's Concert, 125 m (410 ft) underground in the mind-boggling UNESCO-protected salt mines in Wieliczka. ⓦ www.kopalnia.pl

February
Shanties Landlocked Krakow hosts the annual International Festival of Sailors' Music. ⓦ www.shanties.pl

March

Bach Days Inside one of the city's best-kept secrets, Florianka Hall.
ⓐ Ul Basztowa 8 ⓣ 012 422 51 73 ⓦ www.amuz.krakow.pl

Jazz in Krakow A week-long celebration, featuring performers from all over the world. ⓦ www.jazz.krakow.pl

May

Great Dragon Parade Outdoor events including concerts, firework displays and flying dragons in the Rynek and other locations. ⓦ www.groteska.pl

Museum Night Cut-price entry to over 20 museums for one night only. Highlights include an after-dark adventure in the Botanical Gardens and the Night of the Hassidim in Kazimierz's Old Synagogue. ⓦ www.cracowonline.com

🔺 *Step into spring in Wawel*

Krakow Film Festival The oldest film festival in Poland, showcasing Polish and international shorts and feature-length films of all genres. Ⓦ www.cracowfilmfestival.pl

June
Krakow Opera Summer Starting in June and running until the end of August, the city's opera season comes alive with a series of summer concerts. ☏ 012 628 91 01 Ⓦ www.opera.krakow.pl
Ulica Józefa Feast A one-day street party along Kazimierz's ul Józefa. Ⓦ www.cracowonline.com
Wianki *Wianki* are candlelit wreaths the young maidens of Krakow float down the Wisła River as part of the all-night merrymaking and bonfire parties on St John's Day on 24 June. Since the 19th century the ancient pagan festival has been the scene of a huge fiesta, with fireworks and live music along the river close to Wawel.

July
International Festival of Street Theatre Three days of fire-eating, magic and exotic street performances in the Rynek featuring theatre groups from all over the world. Ⓦ www.teatrkto.pl
Jewish Festival of Culture The big one (see page 14).

August
Pierogi Festival Sample one of the country's favourite national dishes around the city. Ⓦ www.cracowonline.com

September
Dachshund Parade Owners of one of the world's most favourite

hounds converge in the old town for one glorious day every September to show off their sausage dogs.
Ⓦ www.cracowonline.com

October
Organ Days A three-day celebration of an instrument intrinsically linked with Krakow. Ⓦ www.filharmonia.krakow.pl

December
Christmas Cribs Competition The morning of the first Thursday of the month sees a presentation of the best of the year's famous Christmas cribs in the Rynek.

PUBLIC HOLIDAYS
New Year's Day 1 Jan
Easter Sunday 4 Apr 2010; 24 Apr 2011; 15 Apr 2012
Easter Monday 5 Apr 2010; 25 Apr 2011; 16 Apr 2012
Labour Day 1 May
Constitution Day 3 May
Assumption 15 Aug
All Saints' Day 1 Nov
Independence Day 11 Nov
Christmas Day 25 Dec (Christmas Eve is celebrated more than Christmas Day, and is the traditional day for eating Christmas dinner – usually carp. Strangely, Christmas Eve is not a public holiday, whereas Christmas Day is.)

Jewish Festival of Culture

An established fixture on Krakow's annual cultural calendar, the city's huge Jewish Festival of Culture was started in 1988 somewhat controversially by the Roman Catholic Janusz Makuch. Initially a rather bookish event that attempted to bring Polish and Jewish cultures together through intellectual discussion, the festival has ballooned into one of the biggest Jewish cultural events in the world. Attracting visitors and participants from all corners of the globe, the city's traditional Jewish quarter of Kazimierz and the old town are transformed for almost a fortnight into a non-stop celebration of a culture whose followers, up until World War II, made up a quarter of Krakow's population.

As well as a barrage of events for spectators, from poetry recitals to some of the best Klezmer music you're ever likely to hear, the festival provides visitors with scores of opportunities to get involved. Helping keep ancient Jewish traditions alive, a range of workshops take place on such diverse subjects as Hassidic dancing, paper cutting, kosher cooking and Hebrew calligraphy. Most of the events are free to attend and many of them are available to English speakers. The festival finishes in spectacular style with a massive free outdoor concert in Kazimierz's ul Szeroka, attracting over 10,000 people who come to listen to music on a huge stage outside the Old Synagogue and sample some fine Jewish food.

Despite cries from some that the festival is nothing more than a clever marketing ploy to exploit Jewish culture and tradition, it continues to grow in size and variety annually. Taking place during Krakow's hottest month, July, the Jewish

Festival of Culture is a truly remarkable event that's more than worth attending.

Festival office @ Ul Józefa 36 @ 012 431 15 17
@ www.jewishfestival.pl

⬤ *Musical performance at the Jewish Festival*

History

Archaeologists believe the Krakow area was inhabited as far back as 50,000 BC, when a small industrial settlement making primitive tools existed on what's now Wawel Hill. One of the oldest cities in Poland, Krakow was already a thriving Slavic trading city when it was incorporated into the Piast dynasty in around AD 990 and is believed by many to be the birthplace of the modern Polish nation. With the establishment of the bishopric of Krakow in AD 1000 and the construction of Wawel Cathedral soon after, Krakow's fate as an important city was sealed.

In 1038 Krakow became the capital of Poland, a status that lasted until 1596 when the royal court was moved to Warsaw. Although Polish kings and queens continued to be buried in Krakow the city soon entered a period of decline. During the 18th century Krakow fell victim to a series of sieges and occupations, caught in the middle of the battles for supremacy between Russia, Prussia and Austria. In 1795 Krakow became part of the latter, before a brief period inside Napoleon's Duchy of Warsaw (1807–15) and another interlude as an independent republic (1815–46).

Absorbed back into the Austrian empire in 1846, Krakow became a thriving centre of Polish culture, and the birthplace of the movement for national revival. After independence in 1918 the city became one of the most culturally and politically important cities in the region. On 6 September 1939 the Germans invaded Krakow, wiping out over 700 years of Jewish culture. Poland fell into the communist sphere of influence until 1989. Stalin once famously said that forcing communism on the Poles was like trying to put a saddle on a cow, a statement evidenced by the fact that Poland was the only country behind the Iron Curtain where religious activity was allowed to flourish unhindered.

The construction of the socialist realist Nowa Huta in the 1950s, an act that was intended to deeply humiliate the religious and conservative population of Krakow, backfired badly, and it was from this district that some of the most outspoken and violent episodes against communist rule came. Krakow's proudest moment arrived in 1978 when its charismatic archbishop, Karol Wojtyla, became Pope John Paul II. With his spiritual and occasional active backing, the threads of communism began to unwind, and by 1989 the country was free again. Now Poland's number one tourist attraction, Krakow has seen enormous changes during the last decade. After months of speculation, in September 2008 Prime Minister Donald Tusk announced that Poland will adopt the euro in 2011, assuming that inflation can be kept under control.

⏺ *The interior of Wawel Cathedral. Catholicism is central to Polish history*

Lifestyle

The cradle of Polish science, art, music and religion, Krakow has a population that is famous for its conservative and religious temperament. The presence of its ancient university has at the same time created a contradictory atmosphere in which open debate, new experiences and a desire to learn about other cultures are equally important. Notoriously careful with their money, Krakow's thrifty inhabitants know

KRAKOW & THE POPE

Ever since the founding of the first cathedral on Wawel Hill in the 11th century, the citizens of Krakow and the Polish people in general have looked to the Catholic Church for a sense of national unity. Catholicism has been the guiding light through numerous historical calamities, most recently playing a pivotal role in the underground resistance movement against the communist authorities. The late Pope John Paul II, the former archbishop of Krakow and the first non-Italian pontiff in over 400 years, is genuinely believed by the Poles to have been a key influence behind the collapse of socialism, and remains an enormous source of pride. His death shocked the nation in ways impossible for an outsider to comprehend. When attempting to untangle the many complexities and inconsistencies of the people of Krakow, it's a good idea to bear this in mind.

🔺 *Eating out and socialising are a way of life in Krakow*

how to have a good time without reaching too far inside their pockets, and, once you get to know them a little better, provide newcomers with a source of deep and affectionate friendship that will last a lifetime. Great lovers of culture, the good people of Krakow are fond of the theatre, and consider visiting art galleries, attending live music performances and eating out a national duty. It's thanks to this quality that Krakow can boast one of the liveliest cultural scenes in the country.

With plenty of mountain air in their blood, the locals are deeply attached to nature and take every available opportunity to disappear to the countryside, where many people keep a second home. This is particularly common during August, the traditional month for holidays, when many businesses close their doors and parts of the city resemble a ghost town.

Culture

From Yiddish theatre to sausage dog parades, Krakow is an astonishingly diverse cultural city. Boasting some 30 major theatrical venues, world-class art and Poland's best selection of museums, Krakow offers more culture than many cities twice its size.

Modern Polish theatre began in the 19th century when Krakow was one of the main centres of modernist art in Eastern Europe. Contemporary productions by international playwrights inspired many nationals, including Stanisław Wyspiański (see page 22), who wrote a total of 37 plays, including *Wesele* (*The Wedding*), arguably Poland's greatest, adapted for cinema in 1973 by the Oscar-winning director Andrzej Wajda. Among the city's great theatres are the Groteska Puppet, Mask & Actor Theatre, which stages productions for both children and adults, the Juliusz Słowacki Theatre and the Stary Teatr (Old Theatre), Poland's first.

Krakow has never produced a great composer, although this hasn't stopped it from being a centre of great music for centuries, from Klezmer to opera to the diverse repertoire of Nowa Huta's multiple award-winning Steelworks Brass Band. Musical highlights include a visit to the Opera Krakówska, Krakow Filharmonia and Kazimierz's predominantly Jewish-themed Krakow Opera Kameralna.

National icon and Krakow native Jan Matejko (1838–93), Stanisław Wyspiański's teacher, painted bombastic oil paintings depicting historical events, many of which can be seen in the house that bears his name in the old town. As well as the many historical masterpieces, insight into the 21st-century Polish creative psyche can be found inside galleries throughout Krakow, including the Palace of Art and the small gallery above the Pauza bar (see page 77).

⬤ *The opulent Juliusz Słowacki Theatre*

WYSPIAŃSKI

Architect, painter, playwright and poet, Krakow's creative genius was unquestionably Stanisław Wyspiański (1869–1907). A leading member of the Polish revival *Młoda Polska* (Young Poland) movement, Wyspiański's output was immense. Blending tradition and modernism, he is perhaps best remembered for his fanciful art nouveau stained-glass designs that grace several buildings around the city and are mentioned throughout this guidebook. Like all good artistic heroes, Stanisław Wyspiański suffered from both physical and mental illness, and died at the tragically young age of 38. His body lies at rest in the city's Pauline Church (see page 83). The museum opened in his honour (see page 70) is a good place to find out more.

The highlight for most art lovers is the Czartoryski Museum, home to Leonardo da Vinci's *Lady with an Ermine*, a rare example of an oil painting by the great man. The diversity and quality of museums in the city will tempt you to make a significant dent in your budget. To get the most out of them, visit during February's extraordinary Museum Night (see page 11) or buy a Krakow Card (see page 46).

● *Chillies and garlic for sale in the old town*

Shopping

The first and for some the most important thing to know about shopping in Krakow and Poland in general is that alcohol and cigarettes are cheaper in the street than they are in duty free. Clambering off a 737 clutching a carrier bag full of vodka and Rothmans with a big grin on your face cuts no ice here. Beyond that, the general retail experience is much the same as it is in any other European city. Of course, there are exceptions. Notably, the fabulous market in Kazimierz (see page 46) and the extraordinary shops selling religious items of every persuasion scattered around the old town. For specific and in-depth coverage of shopping in Krakow, see the relevant 'Retail therapy' sections in this book.

The combination of an emerging middle class and a proliferation of people with disposable incomes has led to a mushrooming of shopping malls all over Krakow. Hardly indicative of traditional Polish culture, malls do at least show the general state of the modern nation, which up until recently had to make do with limited goods of poor quality endorsed by the state. Given the often appalling weather conditions during the winter months, malls, as much as you want to hate them, are a welcome introduction to Krakow's shopping scene.

Galeria Centrum Just off the Rynek. The oldest and least ostentatious of the bunch. More of a department store than a mall really. ⓐ Ul św Anny 2 ⓣ 012 422 98 22 ⓛ 09.30–20.30 Mon–Fri, 10.00–20.00 Sat, 10.00–17.00 Sun

Galeria Kazimierz Complete with a multiplex cinema, this beauty is the only mall in the centre offering entertainment as

◆ *Icon shopping in the Cloth Hall*

USEFUL SHOPPING PHRASES

What time do the shops open/close?
O której godzinie otwierają/zamykają sklepy?
O ktoo-rey go-jee-nyair otvyerayom/za-me-ka-yom skhle-pe?

How much is this?
Ile to kosztuje?
Ee-lair toh ko-shtoo-yeh?

Can I try this on?
Czy mogę to przymierzyć?
Che mo-ghair toh pshe-mye-jech?

My size is ...
Mój rozmiar to ...
Mooy roz-myarh toh ...

I'll take this one please
Poproszę o to
Po-pro-sheh o toh

This is too large/too small/too expensive.
Do you have any others?
To jest zbyt duże/zbyt małe/zbyt drogie.
Czy macie coś in-ne-go?
Toh yest zbit doo-jeh/zbit ma-weh/zbit dro-ghyeh.
Che ma-che cosh in-ne-go?

well as shopping. ⓐ Ul Podgórska 34 ⓣ 012 433 01 01
ⓛ 10.00–22.00 Mon–Sat, 10.00–20.00 Sun
Galeria Krakowska A huge beast next to the train station,
bursting with glitzy shops and fast-food outlets. ⓐ Ul Pawia 5
ⓣ 012 428 99 00 ⓦ www.galeria-krakowska.pl ⓛ 09.00–22.00
Mon–Sat, 10.00–21.00 Sun

Eating & drinking

People don't come to Krakow for the fine dining. With few exceptions, the Poles still haven't got the hang of cooking anything but their own food, which is thankfully both varied and delicious. Eating in Krakow is a mostly ad-hoc affair anyway, an obligatory chore fitted in somewhere between waking up and falling off a barstool. As well as the local food and drink listed below, look out for *pierogi*, a ravioli-type dish served with sour cream instead of tomato sauce and sold in all Polish and many international restaurants. Most staff working in restaurants in the old town speak English and will be able to advise you on what local dishes are on offer.

Picnics are a good summer option, with the Planty (see page 72) and Botanical Gardens (see page 98) offering two excellent places in which to eat under the sky. Despite its profusion of tourists, the centre of Krakow is a heavily populated residential area, with small supermarkets on every street that can provide all the necessary requirements.

As you'll soon notice, there are a lot of small stalls around selling different varieties of bread. The most common is the

PRICE CATEGORIES

The following price ratings used throughout this guidebook indicate the average price per head for a two- or three-course meal excluding drinks.

£ up to 30 zł ££ 30–60 zł £££ over 60 zł

precel, a bagel-shaped, plain or seeded white roll, sold for between 1 zł and 1.50 zł. The other ubiquitous pseudo roll is the *oscypek*. Bearing an uncanny resemblance to a fancy bread roll, *oscypek* is actually a smoked, salty goat's milk cheese. Originating from the nearby mountains, *oscypki* aren't everyone's cup of tea, but they do provide the perfect accompaniment to the *precel*, forming the fundamental ingredients for snacking on the hoof or in a park. Sometimes available hot and even offered in miniature versions, a large *oscypek* will set you back around 10 zł.

◆ *Grab an* oscypek *and you might get a surprise*

Polish desserts, notably *kremówka* (cream-filled cakes), are worth the plane fare alone. Rumours are that the late Pope John Paul II's final trip to Krakow in 1999 was heavily influenced by the lack of *kremówka* in the Vatican. Sold in many cafés, and in shops by weight, a large piece of *tofinka* (a kind of sweet cake) should be packed in all picnic baskets as standard.

Krakow is reputed to possess the highest concentration of pubs in the world, a strange fact considering that Poland's beer is not generally referred to with awe; Polish vodka on the other hand is up there with the best of the bunch. Brands to watch out for are the aristocratic Chopin and Belvedere, and the more bucolic Żubrowka, which comes with a blade of grass in every bottle. The other indigenous tipple of note is *Grzaniec Galicyjski*, a locally produced herbal wine that's drunk scorching hot. Savouring any of the above in a public place could result in a sizeable fine or even some unplanned rehab. Polish police are not renowned for their toleration of public inebriation: if you are arrested for being drunk in a public place, you risk being committed to a drying out clinic from which you will not be released until you are sober, and whose fees you will be responsible for paying.

As Poland becomes more westernised, the propensity to tip is definitely on the increase. Considering the average restaurant employee in Krakow is lucky to take home more than 800 zł (around £170) every month, you may like to help the new trend along. The accepted norm is to give ten per cent or round up the bill. Finally, one word of warning: saying thank you to your waiter or waitress as you pay is interpreted as an open invitation to pocket the change.

USEFUL DINING PHRASES

I would like a table for ... people
Poproszę o stolik dla ... osób
Po-pro-sheh o sto-leek dla ... o-soob

Waiter/waitress!
Kelner/Kelnerka!
Kelner/Kelnerka!

May I have the bill please?
Poproszę o rachunek?
Po-pro-sheh o ra-hoo-neck?

Could I have it well cooked/medium/rare please?
Poproszę o dobrze/średnio/lekko wysmażone?
Po-pro-sheh o do-bjeh/shre-dnyo/lek-ko ve-sma-jo-ne?

I am a vegetarian. Does this contain meat?
Jetsem wegetarianinem/wegetarianką (fem.).
Czy w tym daniu jest mięso?
Yestem vegetarianinem/vegetariankahng (fem.).
Tchee fteem dah-nyoo yest myensoh?

Excuse me, where is the toilet?
Przepraszam, gdzie jest toaleta?
Pshe-pra-sham, ghjair yest toe-a-lair-tah?

Entertainment & nightlife

Bursting with bearded eccentrics in jazz clubs and scantily clad partygoers in places that sometimes forget to close, Krakow is a hedonist's dream. The distinction between bars and clubs is a little blurred at times, with many places claiming to be a bar hosting all-night sessions where dancing on the tables is considered good form. In short, if you can't find something to do after the sun dips behind the gargoyles of the Cloth Hall then you've almost certainly been locked in a church.

The old town is the main place to go clubbing and also boasts the highest concentration of bars, although Kazimierz can claim the more interesting selection of the latter. *Krakow In Your Pocket* (Ⓦ www.inyourpocket.com) has great coverage of the city's nightlife. It's available all around town and can be picked up for free from some hotel lobbies. Table service is the norm in most bars. One word of warning: if you walk past a place that says Night Club, especially outside the city centre, it could well be a brothel.

While in Krakow it would be unforgivable not to sample the city's jazz scene:

Boogie One of the best in town, with a sophisticated feel and some fine performances. ⓐ Ul Szpitalna 9 ⓣ 012 429 43 06 Ⓦ www.boogiecafe.pl Ⓛ 10.00–02.00

Harris Piano Jazz Bar A smoky underground club with no air conditioning. A classic among jazz clubs. ⓐ Rynek Główny 28 ⓣ 012 421 57 41 Ⓦ www.harris.krakow.pl Ⓛ 09.00–02.00

U Muniaka A labyrinth of rooms hide the occasional well-known face, including Krakow resident Nigel Kennedy. ⓐ Ul Floriańska 3 ⓣ 012 423 12 05 Ⓛ 19.00–02.00

Piec'Art The preserve of the city's better class of jazz hooligan inside a tip-top old-town venue. ⓐ Ul Szewska 12 ⓣ 012 429 64 25 ⓦ www.piecart.pl ⓒ 13.00–02.00

Stalowe Magnolie An extraordinary labyrinth of opulence in a pricey and sophisticated venue that puts on quality live music every night. ⓐ Ul św. Jana 15 ⓣ 012 422 84 72

◔ *A fire dancer lights up the old town*

ⓦ www.stalowemagnolie.com ⓛ 18.00–02.00 Sun–Thur, 18.00–04.00 Fri & Sat

Krakow is the city in which the failed fireman Krzysztof Kieślowski started his illustrious cinematic career, and where going to the cinema is something the locals like to do a lot. Films are shown in their original language with Polish subtitles. Tickets cost 10–20 zł.

ARS Hollywood blockbusters and the occasional art house treat in the heart of the city. ⓐ Ul św Jana 6 ⓣ 012 421 41 99 ⓦ www.ars.pl

IMAX A monster of a screen. ⓐ Al Pokoju 44 ⓣ 012 290 90 90 ⓝ Tram: 1, 14, 22; Bus: 125

Kino Pod Baranami One of the city's few remaining art house cinemas and the spiritual home of November's Independent Film Festival. ⓐ Rynek Główny 27 ⓣ 012 423 07 68 ⓦ www.kinopodbaranami.pl

TICKETS

With the exception of major imported acts, ticket prices are low in Poland. Many events in Krakow sell out fast, so buying in advance is highly recommended. For most events such as special club nights, jazz concerts and cinema screenings, tickets should be bought from the venue in question. Theatre and concert tickets can be bought from venues, or from the friendly, English-speaking staff at the **Cultural Information Centre** (ⓐ Ul św Jana 2 ⓣ 012 421 77 87 ⓦ www.karnet.krakow.pl ⓛ 10.00–18.00).

Sport & relaxation

SPECTATOR SPORTS
Football
Two of Poland's oldest and most successful teams play
in Krakow, although most people prefer to watch them on
television due to the legendary violence on the terraces.
Tickets cost buttons and are bought at the ground if you
think you're hard enough.
Cracovia ⓐ Kałuży 1 ❶ 012 427 35 62 ⓦ www.cracovia.pl
Ⓝ Tram: 15, 18; Bus: 109, 134, 409
Wisła ⓐ Reymonta 22 ❶ 012 623 95 95 ⓦ www.wisla.krakow.pl
Ⓝ Tram: 15, 18

PARTICIPATION SPORTS
Cycling
Two Wheels A day's rental costs around 30 zł; bring your
passport or driver's licence and a 200 zł deposit. ⓐ Ul Józefa 5
❶ 012 421 57 85 ⓦ www.dwakola.neostrada.pl ❷ 10.00–18.00
Mon–Fri, 10.00–14.00 Sat

Extreme sports
Reni Sport Climbing walls, the real thing (including professional
training) in the Tatra Mountains, plus other nutty things to
do including the inevitable bungee jumping. ⓐ Ul Czepca 11
❶ 012 638 07 34 ⓦ www.renisport.pl Ⓝ Tram: 4, 8, 13; Bus: 601

▶ *Hiring a bike is a great way to see the city*

Golf
Krakow Valley Golf & Country Club An 18-hole course 40 km (25 miles) west of Krakow, plus driving range, hotel, conference centre and horse-riding facilities. A one-way taxi trip costs around 100 zł. ⓐ Krzeszowice 3, Paczółtowice ⓣ 012 282 94 67 ⓦ www.krakow-valley.com

Swimming
Park Wodny The undisputed king of swimming pools, with water slides, health and beauty facilities and a decent café. ⓐ Ul Dobrego Pasterza 126 ⓣ 012 616 31 90 ⓦ www.parkwodny.pl ⓝ Bus: 125, 128, 129, 132, 138, 139, 142, 152, 169, 188

Winter sports
If you don't want to travel to Zakopane (see page 116), the city's indoor ice skating rink is a good choice:
Lodowisko Krakowianka Two rinks, home to the local professional ice-hockey team. Skate rental available. ⓐ Ul Siedleckiego 7 ⓣ 012 421 13 17 ⓛ 10.00–19.00 ⓝ Tram: 1, 4, 5, 7, 9, 10, 11, 14, 15, 22, 32, 40, 44; Bus: 128, 184

Accommodation

Even though prices creep up every year, the cost of hotel accommodation in Krakow remains laughable in comparison to the West. This not only makes the city an attractive budget option, but also means visitors can afford to base themselves in a more central location. However, the old town can be rowdy at night, and consequently not much fun for many, including those travelling with children. Likewise, hostels can be noisy affairs. If you're looking for a good night's sleep in the centre, choose something just a little further out.

HOSTELS
Good Bye Lenin £ A standard hostel experience, the communist theme is fun but really little more than a cheap marketing gimmick. ➌ Ul Joselewicza 23 (Further afield) ☎ 012 421 20 30 🌐 www.goodbyelenin.pl

PRICE CATEGORIES
The following price ratings used throughout this guidebook indicate the average price per double room, including breakfast, per night. Prices are subject to change depending on whether you book during the high or low season. In Zakopane, the high season includes the period roughly between Christmas and the end of February.
£ up to 150 zł   ££ 150–300 zł   £££ over 300 zł

Lemon Hostel £ A ten-minute walk from the old town, Lemon Hostel offers a pleasant environment with rooms named after fruit. ⓐ Ul Grabowskiego 6 (Further afield) ⓣ 012 633 51 48 ⓦ www.lemonhostel.pl

Mama's £ With a distinctly feminine feel, keeping things basic here means the great location is affordable for all. ⓐ Ul Bracka 4 (The old town & Wawel) ⓣ 012 429 59 40 ⓦ www.mamashostel.com.pl

Nathan's Villa £ This infamous little venture offers good service and all-night parties in the basement. ⓐ Ul św Agnieszki 1 (Further afield) ⓣ 012 422 35 45 ⓦ www.nathansvilla.com

Seventh Heaven £ Bright colours and tatty furniture are the order of the day here. Very popular with English-speaking backpackers and budget travellers. ⓐ Ul Lenartowicza 7 (Further afield) ⓣ 012 633 38 87 ⓦ www.seventhheaven.pl

Hostel Rynek 7 ££ One of the best addresses in Krakow. Relaxed, with the larger dormitories offering spectacular views of the Rynek. ⓐ Rynek Główny 7/6 (The old town & Wawel) ⓣ 012 431 16 98 ⓦ www.hostelrynek7.pl

APARTMENTS

Affinity Flats ££–£££ Heaps of stylish and well-renovated apartments throughout the city, from modest accommodation in grey blocks to the ultimate luxury pad in the old town. ⓐ Ul Karmelicka 7 (Locations throughout the city, office in Further

⬤ Hotel Saski is situated in the thick of things

afield) ☎ 012 428 72 00 ⓦ www.affinityflats.com

Red Brick Apartments ££–£££ Offering a great location just
west of the train station and north of the Old Town, this classy
establishment provides 16 magnificent apartments, including
kitchens and wireless internet. A touch pricey, but worth
every penny. ⓐ Ul Kurniki 3 (Further afield) ☎ 012 628 66 00
ⓦ www.redbrick.pl

HOTELS

2nd Floor ££ Plastic furniture and pink pillowcases for the
discerning gay budget traveller. A recommended introduction
into the still very much nascent world of gay Krakow. Note that
there's no breakfast provided here, but a small kitchen is available
free of charge for guests. Also note that it really only caters to
gay guests. ⓐ Ul Nowowiejska 4 (Further afield) ☎ 012 294 56 99
ⓦ www.2ndfloor.queer.pl

Hotel Saski ££ A fabulous option for those looking for a
relatively cheap sleep in the old town, Saski offers rococo
splashes, an antique lift and a bit of money left in your pocket
to explore the choice of quality restaurants along the street
it's located on. ⓐ Ul Sławkowska 3 (The old town & Wawel)
☎ 012 421 42 22 ⓦ www.hotelsaski.com.pl

Monopol ££ A nicely renovated hotel immediately east of the
old town, popular with tour groups and featuring all manner
of extras including good facilities for disabled travellers and
the option of bringing your pet with you if you can't bear to

be parted. ⓐ Ul św Gertrudy 6 (Further afield) ⓣ 012 422 76 66
ⓦ www.rthotels.com.pl

Wielopole ££ A choice of excellent-value singles, doubles and
triples a couple of minutes east of the old town. The rooms
are basic but clean, the buffet breakfast in the basement is
better than many, and the staff seem to be under the distinct
impression that you're paying five times the price you really are
for your room. ⓐ Ul Wielopole 3 (Further afield) ⓣ 012 422 14 75
ⓦ www.wielopole.pl

Pollera £££ Close to the train and bus stations, Pollera's classy
art nouveau chic comes with a price, but the combination of
location, impeccable service and the fabulous Wyspiański stained-
glass window on the staircase makes this one a tempting offer
for travellers looking to push the boat out a bit while taking in
the sites and sensations of the city. ⓐ Szpitalna 30 (The old town
& Wawel) ⓣ 012 422 10 44 ⓦ www.pollera.com.pl

Stary £££ A perfect blend of medieval elegance and modern
charm, if you're in Krakow on business at somebody else's
expense or you've just won the lottery you couldn't do much
better than this place. The perfect 5-star experience, including
a swimming pool in the cellar and a great rooftop bar in the
summer with superb views of the old town. ⓐ Ul Szczepańska 5
(The old town & Wawel) ⓣ 012 384 08 08 ⓦ www.stary.hotel.com.pl

THE BEST OF KRAKOW

Whether you're planning a flying visit or staying longer
to savour the city, there's more than enough to hold
your interest in Krakow. The following sights, places
and experiences should not be missed.

TOP 10 ATTRACTIONS

- **Wawel** The spiritual home of the Polish nation, this
  breathtaking ensemble of buildings justifies Krakow's
  reputation as one of the most beautiful cities in Europe
  (see page 69)

- **St Mary's Basilica** The mind-boggling interior of St Mary's
  mirrors perfectly the deeply religious essence of Poland
  and its people (see page 66)

- **Archdiocesan Museum** Evokes the spirit and the legend
  of the young Polish sports fan who went on to become
  Pope John Paul II (see page 60)

- **Cloth Hall** Where Lenin once drank tea and brewed a
  revolution, and now home to arguably the best-located
  tourist market in Europe (see page 64)

⬇ *Paintings for sale on the walls of the Barbican*

- **Remuh Cemetery** The city's oldest surviving Jewish cemetery is a poignant place in which to start unravelling the tale of an ancient culture that was wiped out in the flicker of an eye (see page 82)

- **Da Vinci** A trip to the extraordinary Czartoryski Museum offers visitors a rare glimpse of one of the world's few Leonardo da Vinci masterpieces (see page 64)

- **Lazy afternoons in the Planty** Pack a Polish picnic and head for the shade of the fabulously green and peaceful city centre park (see page 72)

- **Traditional Polish restaurant** Try the fairytale adventure for gourmands as provided by the unforgettable U Babci Maliny (see page 73)

- **Discovering Wyspiański** Explore Krakow's abundance of art nouveau stained-glass masterpieces bequeathed to the city by the late Stanisław Wyspiański (see page 22)

- **Kazimierz's bric-à-brac** Spend a few hours rifling through the flea markets, antique shops and the amazing market in Kazimierz (see page 46)

Suggested itineraries

HALF-DAY: KRAKOW IN A HURRY

Head for the Rynek, pick up a daft souvenir in the Cloth Hall,
then spend a few minutes contemplating the masterpieces
inside St Mary's Basilica. If you need refreshment, enjoy one
of the square's cafés and watch the world go by before taking
a wander around the rest of the area, popping into a museum
if time allows.

1 DAY: TIME TO SEE A LITTLE MORE

As well as the above recommendations, take time to explore
the majesty of Wawel Cathedral before heading south for a
tour of the old Jewish area of Kazimierz. Don't miss the Remuh
Synagogue and attached cemetery, and be sure to take some
time to visit the poignant exhibitions at the nearby Galicia
Jewish Museum. If you've got more time, spend 30 minutes
or more inside the amazing Ethnographic Museum before
finishing the evening in a traditional Jewish restaurant followed
by beer in one of Kazimierz's wacky bars.

2–3 DAYS: TIME TO SEE MUCH MORE

Add to the above itinerary the full Wawel experience, itself
a day's work if you do it properly, and use up the rest of the
time to make the most of Krakow's museums. Explore the
sights of the Jewish ghetto in Podgórze and get out to Nowa
Huta if you can. Use your evenings to sample the best of the
city's restaurants, bars and clubs.

LONGER: ENJOYING KRAKOW TO THE FULL

Precisely what this guidebook's been written for. Get the most out of the best Krakow has to offer, including a leisurely adventure in Nowa Huta and a night or two in Zakopane.

🔺 *Under the arches, Krakow central market*

Something for nothing

A few days in Krakow are hardly going to make a large dent in your wallet, but it's still nice to be able to enjoy the city without having to pay for the pleasure. The most obvious way of getting something for nothing is to explore Krakow's many churches. With the exception of St Mary's Basilica, all of the churches in the old town are free to enter. Remember that men should remove their hats when entering a Catholic church (the complete reverse for a synagogue), and keep their legs and, if possible, arms covered. Women are only expected to cover their shoulders. Most museums open their doors for free on one day of the week, which, if you pack a few in, can save you a fair amount of cash.

The higgledy-piggledy jumble of buildings in Kazimierz offers a wealth of opportunities to browse an amazing array of junk, old communist-era consumer goods, antiques, fur coats and much more in an ever-increasing number of shops. The

KRAKOW CARD
Available in both two-day (50 zł) and three-day (65 zł) versions, the Krakow Card gives users free access to over 30 museums plus unlimited travel on the city's public transport system. Like other similar cards, it also offers discounts in shops and restaurants. Available at the Cultural Information Centre (see page 33).
ⓦ www.krakowcard.com

extraordinary old Jewish market offers a different experience every day, from clothes to cabbages to a brilliant, large **Saturday market** (❸ Plac Nowy ◷ 05.30–15.00 summer; 05.30–12.30 winter) featuring the best selection of bric-à-brac in the city.

If you've already bought one of the recommended books listed on page 137, you could do a lot worse than take advantage of the city walks included in them. Covering some of the more obscure sights in the old town, Kazimierz and Nowa Huta, these really well-thought-out tours can add a whole new dimension to the city.

◔ Kazimierz market, a browser's paradise

When it rains

There are a million things to do if it rains in Krakow, from delving deep underground in Wawel Cathedral's extraordinary crypts and the Dragon's Cave to just sitting and watching the world go by in a café. Perhaps the best way to use up a few wet hours is to take advantage of some of the less well-known museums in the city

Among the countless exhibits at the **Archaeology Museum** (ⓐ Ul Poselska 3 ① 012 422 71 00) are some particularly interesting models of life in Małopolska as it was lived during the Stone Age, an exceptional collection of reproductions of the type of clothing worn in the region from 70,000 BC until the founding of the old town, and a mysterious assortment of artefacts from ancient Egypt.

Nathan of Nathan's Villa fame (see page 38) has taken his hobby into the public realm and opened a large aquarium inside the glorious surroundings of the city's former Natural History Museum, naming it **Krakow Aquarium** (ⓐ Ul św. Sebastiana 9 ① 012 429 10 49 ⓦ www.aquariumkrakow.com). Although some of the old museum's exhibits are still on display upstairs, including the legendary Ice Age hairy mammoth, most of the building has been taken over by tanks full of sharks, exotic reptiles and other eerie beasts. Aimed at children but of interest to all, many of the exhibits come with computer-aided presentations and there's even the option of special guided tours. Even if reptiles aren't exactly up your street, the magnificent art nouveau surroundings are worth a look at in themselves.

Located inside a wonderful 15th-century building, Krakow's brilliant **Pharmacy Museum** (ⓐ Ul Floriańska 25 ⓣ 012 421 92 79 ⓦ www.muzeumfarmacji.pl) includes all manner of exhibits from full-scale reproductions of ancient apothecary shops to some beastly snakes in jars and, on the top floor, a really good display of traditional herbal medicines. Also of interest is the small exhibit dedicated to the extraordinary and brave Pole, Tadeusz Pankiewicz (see the Museum of National Remembrance on page 95).

🔺 *Escape the rain at the Pharmacy Museum*

On arrival

TIME DIFFERENCE
Poland's clocks are on Central European Time (CET, or GMT+1). During Daylight Saving Time (late Mar–Oct), the clocks are put ahead one hour.

ARRIVING
By air
All flights to Krakow arrive at Balice Airport, also known as John Paul II International Airport, 18 km (11 miles) west of the city. Find tourist information, public telephones, ATMs, 24-hour currency exchange and kiosks selling snacks and SIM cards in the combined international arrivals and departures hall. A small terminal immediately northeast of the international terminal deals with all internal flights. The quickest way into town is by taxi, of which the marked **MPT cars** (❶ 91 91) outside the main exit are the cheapest and most reliable (30–50zł into town). The most economical way of getting into the centre is by train. A free bus outside the international terminal building takes you the short trip to the airport's train station. Buy a ticket on board the train (6zł), which travels non-stop to the main train station, Dworzec Główny. The journey time is 15 minutes, and trains run around the clock, every thirty minutes during the day and less frequently at other times.

By rail
Krakow's main train station (Dworzec Główny) remains the least convivial of all three arriving options listed here. Find currency

exchange (🕒 06.00–22.00) and ATMs, plus scores of kiosks selling snacks and SIM cards. The hostel touts who work the train station are almost certainly going to rip you off. Ignore them. Walk the underpass into the Planty and follow the path into the old town, or look around for a taxi if you're travelling further afield.

By road

All international buses arrive at the modern central bus station on ul Bosacka. Facilities are basic, but there are clean toilets, an ATM and a surprisingly good buffet restaurant (🕒 08.00–20.00). The old town is a few hundred metres to the southwest and can be reached by the Magda underpass that goes under the platforms of the central train station next door. Alternatively, taxis are parked outside night and day.

FINDING YOUR FEET

The general pace of life in Krakow is blissfully slow, which, with the exception of when you want something to eat, couldn't be much better. It's safer than most Western European cities too. Beware of the grinning 20-somethings, complete with leather jackets and mongrel dogs, who like to prowl ul Floriańska and the northern part of the Planty looking for beer money. They're harmless but irritating.

ORIENTATION

Most of Krakow's sights and hotels are on the northern shore of the Wisła river, which runs through the city. The old town, Wawel and Kazimierz are all next to each other in a line running

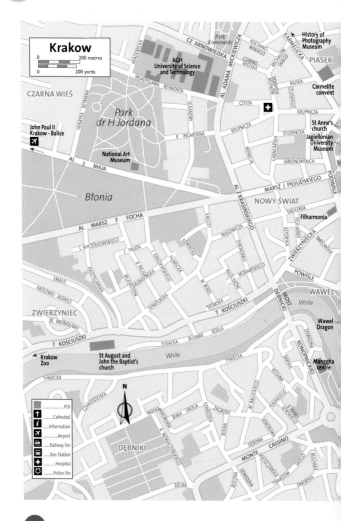

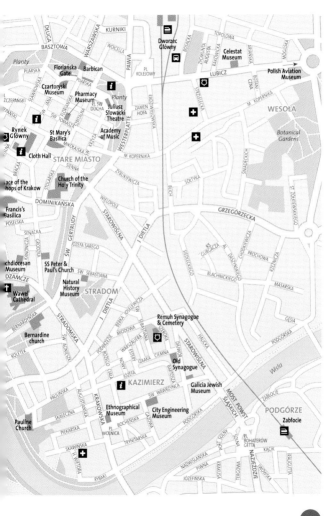

more or less north to south, and can be walked to and from without any problem. The city centre is small enough for you to never worry about getting lost in, but if you do find yourself up a gum tree just ask a local. They don't bite.

GETTING AROUND

Unless you have difficulty walking over relatively short distances or are in Krakow for just a few hours, everything there is to see within the old town and Kazimierz can be seen on foot. For trips further afield, the city's tram service is second to none, and taxis remain a ludicrously cheap way of covering long distances.

Trams

Fast, cheap, efficient, and with the added bonus of being able to slip through the city's increasingly snarling traffic without

🔵 Beat the traffic and take a tram

IF YOU GET LOST, TRY ...

Excuse me, do you speak English?
Przepraszam, czy mówi pan/pani po angielsku?
Pshe-pra-sham, che moo-vee pan/pa-nee poe an-gyels-koo?

Excuse me, is this the right way to the old town/the city centre/the tourist office/the train station/the bus station?
Przepraszam, czy dojdę tędy do starego miasta/centrum miasta/biura turystycznego/dworzec kolejowy/dworca autobusowego?
Pshe-pra-sham, che doy-dair ten-di doe sta-re-go mya-stah/ sten-troom mya-stah/byoo-rah too-ri-sti-chne-go/dvo-zhets ko-le-yo-vi/dvortsah awto-boo-so-vego?

Can you point to it on my map?
Czy móglby pan/moglaby pani pokazać to na mapie?
Che moog-wbe pan/mog-wa-be pa-nee poka-zach na ma-pyair?

hindrance, trams run 05.00–23.00. A single-journey ticket (also valid on buses) costs around 3 zł. Better value are 24-hour (approx 11 zł), 48-hour (approx 19 zł) and 72-hour (25 zł) tickets, which can be bought from kiosks near stops or anywhere you see a 'sprzedaż biletów MPK' sign. Validate your ticket in the machine on board and away you go.

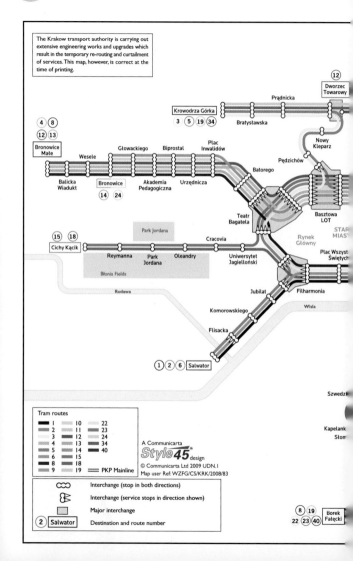

The Krakow transport authority is carrying out extensive engineering works and upgrades which result in the temporary re-routing and curtailment of services. This map, however, is correct at the time of printing.

Dworzec Towarowy (12)

Prądnicka

Krowodrza Górka
3 5 19 34

Bratysławska

Nowy Kleparz

4 8
12 13

Bronowice Małe

Wesele

Głowackiego

Biprostal

Plac Inwalidów

Pędzichów

Batorego

Balicka Wiadukt

Bronowice
14 24

Akademia Pedagogiczna

Urzędnicza

Basztowa LOT

STAR MIAST

Teatr Bagatela

Park Jordana

15 18

Cichy Kącik

Reymanna

Park Jordana

Oleandry

Cracovia

Rynek Główny

Plac Wszyst Świętych

Uniwersytet Jagielloński

Błonia Fields

Rudawa

Jubilat

Filharmonia

Komorowskiego

Wisła

Flisacka

1 2 6 Salwator

Szwedz

Tram routes

■ 1	■ 10	22
■ 2	11	23
3	■ 12	24
■ 4	13	■ 34
5	■ 14	■ 40
■ 6	15	
■ 8	18	
9	19	■ PKP Mainline

A Communicarta
Style 45 design
© Communicarta Ltd 2009 UDN.1
Map user Ref: WZFG/CS/KRK/2008/83

Kapelank
Słom

∞ Interchange (stop in both directions)

Interchange (service stops in direction shown)

☐ Major interchange

2 Salwator Destination and route number

8 19
22 23 40

Borek Fałęcki

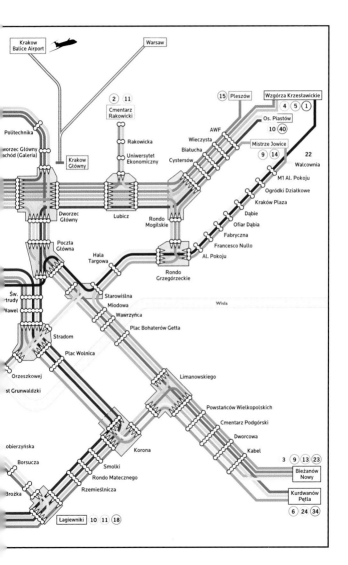

Taxis

Taxis are cheap and form a vital part of the city's after-dark makeup. The standard charge for a taxi ride is around 7zł, with a further 2.50zł or so per kilometre (half-mile) after that. If a taxi has a large sign on the roof with the name and telephone number of the company, you can rest assured that, as long as you make sure the driver switches the meter on before you depart, you won't be ripped off.

Barbakan ☏ 96 61

Metro ☏ 96 67

MPT ☏ 91 91

CAR HIRE

Hiring a car is a waste of money unless you're planning on making excursions outside of the city. As with everywhere else, shopping around secures the best deal. Prices range from 50 zł to 200 zł per day. All of the major car hire companies have offices at the airport.

Avis ⓐ Ul Lubicz 23 ☏ 0601 20 07 02 Ⓦ www.avis.pl

Cracowrent ⓐ Ul Kamieńskiego 41 ☏ 012 265 26 50 Ⓦ www.cracowrent.pl

Hertz ⓐ Al Focha 1 ☏ 012 429 62 62 Ⓦ www.hertz.com.pl

Rentacar ⓐ Ul Piłsudskiego 19 ☏ 012 618 43 30 Ⓦ www.e-rentacar.pl

ⓘ Car crime is rife, so use one of the city's guarded parking areas or choose a hotel with secure parking facilities

---

▶ *Wawel towers above Krakow*

THE CITY OF
Krakow

The old town & Wawel

Saved the indignity of being turned to rubble at the end of
World War II like Poland's other great cities, Krakow's Stare
Miasto (old town) is quite simply flabbergasting. A UNESCO-
protected site since 1978, the old town was founded in 1257
and still retains most of its original features. Laid out in a grid-
like pattern with the huge Rynek Główny (market square) at its
centre, its streets afford the wandering tourist one of the great
pleasures of visiting the city. Wawel, just south of the old town,
is essentially the birthplace of the nation. Both sights deserve
at least some attention before taking advantage of the city's
more modern aspects.

SIGHTS & ATTRACTIONS

Archdiocesan Museum
The one-time home of a young, sports-mad Polish priest called
Karol Wojtyla who went on to become Pope John Paul II, this small
museum containing religious artefacts from the 13th century
onwards is essential visiting for those looking to piece together
the social jigsaw of the city. ❸ Ul Kanonicza 19 ❶ 012 421 89 63
🕙 10.00–16.00 Tues–Fri, 10.00–15.00 Sat & Sun. Admission charge

Barbican
Built around 1498, the Arabesque-inspired Barbican looks like
something out of a fairytale. The seven-turreted structure
features fearsome walls that are 3 m (10 ft) thick, pierced with
130 loopholes, the majority of which are arranged in multiples

of seven, a nod to the then-fashionable science of astronomy; the Barbican was built when there were seven known planets in the solar system. Along with the Floriańska Gate just to the south (circa 1307), the Barbican is by far the best-preserved example of the city's original defences. A plaque on the building's eastern side celebrates the plucky Polish marksman Marcin Oracewicz, who according to legend killed the Russian colonel Panin during the rising of the Confederation of Bar (1768–72) using a button instead of a bullet in his gun. A bust of Oracewicz can be found outside the Celesat Museum (see page 90). ⓐ Ul Basztowa ⓛ 10.30–18.00 May–Oct. Admission charge

⬥ The massive Barbican

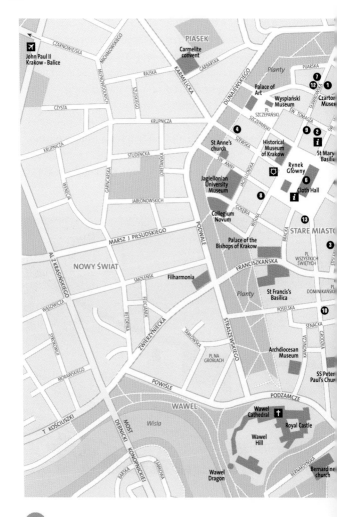

John Paul II
Krakow - Balice

PIASEK

Carmelite
convent

CZARNOWIEJSKA

MICHAŁOWSKIEGO

MINUNOWIGH

RAJSKA

KARMELICKA

GARBARSKA

DUNAJEWSKIEGO

Planty

PUJARSKA

SZUJSKIEGO

CZYSTA

KRUPNICZA

KRUPNICZA

STUDENCKA

LORETANSKA

GARNCARSKA

JABŁONOWSKICH

Palace of
Art

Wyspiański
Museum

PL
SZCZEPAŃSKI

SZCZEPAŃSKA

St Anne's
church

Historical
Museum
of Krakow

SW. ANNY

Jagiellonian
University
Museum

Rynek
Główny

Cloth Hall

Czartor
Musei

SW. TOMASZA

St Mary
Basilii

SW. JANA

GOŁĘBIA

WIŚLNA

BRACKA

Collegium
Novum

STARE MIASTO

MARSZ. J. PIŁSUDSKIEGO

PODWALE

Palace of the
Bishops of Krakow

PL
WSZYSTKICH
ŚWIĘTYCH

AL Z KRASINSKIEGO

NOWY ŚWIAT

FRANCISZKAŃSKA

FELICJANEK

SMOLEŃSK

Filharmonia

Planty

St Francis's
Basilica

PL
DOMINIKAŃSKI

WĄSOWICZA

RETORYKA

ZWIERZYNIECKA

DABŁONSKA

STRASZEWSKIEGO

POSELSKA

SENACKA

SMOLEŃSKA

MORAWSKIEGO

PL NA
GROBLACH

Archdiocesan
Museum

KANONICZA

GRODZKA

SS Peter
Paul's Chur

POWIŚLE

PODZAMCZE

WAWEL

T. KOŚCIUSZKI

MOST
DĘBNICKI

Wisła

Wawel
Cathedral

Royal Castle

KONOPNICKIEJ

BARSKA

ZAMKOWA

SKAWIŃSKA

Wawel
Hill

Wawel
Dragon

Bernardine
church

BERNARDYŃSKA

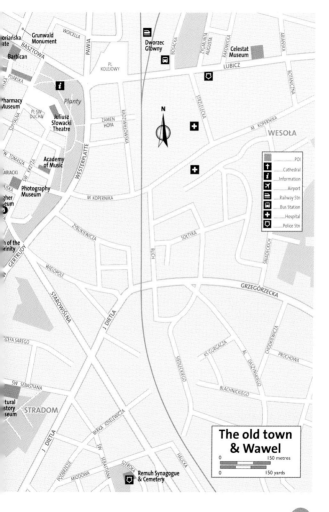

The old town & Wawel

| POI |
| Cathedral |
| Information |
| Airport |
| Railway Stn |
| Bus Station |
| Hospital |
| Police Stn |

Burgher Museum (Hippolit House)

Named after a well-to-do family of 16th-century cloth traders who once lived here, this charming museum features room upon room of recreations of bourgeois living conditions in the city from the 17th to the 20th century. ⓐ Pl Mariacki 3 ⓘ 012 422 42 19 🕐 10.00–17.30 Tues–Sun. Admission charge

Cloth Hall

The imposing Cloth Hall started life as two walls between which local traders would store their goods at night. Its present appearance owes most to the visionary Renaissance labour of the 16th-century Italian architect Giovanni il Mosca (who added the fabulous rooftop gargoyles among other things) and a few neo-Gothic additions in the 19th century. The Cloth Hall was where the local medieval elite came to buy the latest designer fabrics, but it has also seen a variety of other uses. Its most famous patron was none other than Lenin, who was a frequent visitor to the Noworolski café (see page 74) during his stay in the city between 1912 and 1914. The Cloth Hall now plays host to a rather tacky shopping centre, where tourists can pick up overpriced souvenirs from one of many stalls that occupy the colonnade on the ground floor. ⓐ Rynek Główny 1 🕐 10.00–19.00 Mon–Fri, 10.00–18.00 Sat & Sun

Czartoryski Museum

Celebrating both the glories and miseries of human life, a cavalcade of delights can be found tucked away inside this museum. Its main claim to fame is that it houses a Leonardo da Vinci oil painting, *Lady with an Ermine*, one of very few in the

world on show to the public. ⓐ Ul św Jana 19 ⓣ 012 422 55 66
🕒 10.00–18.00 Tues–Sat, 10.00–16.00 Sun. Admission charge

Historical Museum of Krakow

Documenting the life and times of the city from when it received
its royal charter in 1257 until the Nazi invasion of 1939, the museum
highlights include the Fontana Room, designed by the Italian
Baldassare Fontana (1658–1729), and a moving collection of
exhibits celebrating the country's struggle for independence
at the end of World War I. ⓐ Rynek Główny 35 ⓣ 012 619 23 00
🕒 10.00–17.30 Tues–Sun. Admission charge

Jagiellonian University Museum

Founded by King Kazimierz in 1364, the Jagiellonian University
ranks as the third oldest university in Europe. The museum contains
many glorious pieces including the oldest surviving globe to
show the Americas. Guided tours only. Booking recommended.
ⓐ Ul Jagiellońska 15 ⓣ 012 422 05 49 🕒 10.00–15.00 Mon, Wed &
Fri, 10.00–18.00 Tues & Thur, 10.00–14.00 Sat. Admission charge

Rynek Główny

Krakow's undisputed focal point is its main market square Rynek
Główny, or just plain Rynek. Laid out in 1257, the 200 m x 200 m
(656 ft x 656 ft) square was once the largest medieval square
in Europe. Originally the centre of life in the city, the Rynek was
formerly a frenetic bustle of commercial activity, where Jews,
Germans, Poles and others sold their wares. Krakow's post-
communist reinvention of itself has ensured that the Rynek
is once again the city's favourite place to see and be seen in.

As well as its many fine architectural attributes, the Rynek is framed by cafés that sprawl out in the summer, creating the perfect backdrop for a battalion of buskers, horse-drawn carriages, regular summer concerts and a million photographic opportunities.

St Francis's Basilica

First consecrated in 1269, St Francis's is notable as being the first brick building in the city. The current neo-Gothic structure houses some of the finest, if not *the* finest, art nouveau stained glass in Europe, the work of Stanisław Wyspiański (see page 22) produced between 1895 and 1904. ⓐ Pl Wszystkich Świętych, off Franciszkańska ⓣ 012 422 53 76 ⓛ 06.00–20.00

St Mary's Basilica

The basilica owes its present Gothic appearance to building work carried out in the middle of the 14th century; venture inside and you'll be picking your jaw up off the floor. Ablaze with colour and breathtaking sculptures, its centrepiece is the 15th-century altar by the German artist Veit Stoss (Wit Stwosz, 1440–1533). Taking 12 years to complete, Stoss's masterpiece depicts the Virgin Mary's *Quietus* among the apostles and is the largest Gothic altar in Europe. The church's two unequal towers would be fairly unremarkable were it not for the taller one on the left. As well as being open to the public (warning, 239 stairs), an hourly bugle call is made from it around the clock, and has been going on, according to legend, since 1241. ⓐ Rynek Główny 4 ⓣ 012 422 05 21 ⓛ Church: 11.30–18.00 Mon–Fri, 14.00–18.00 Sun. Tower: 09.00–11.30, 13.00–17.30 Tues, Thur & Sat, 3 May–30 Aug. Admission charge for both

⬥ *The two towers of St Mary's Basilica rise above Rynek Główny*

SS Peter & Paul's Church

Having almost fallen down as construction was nearing completion at the start of the 17th century, the baroque SS Peter & Paul's Church (Kościól św Piotra i Pawła) has been dicing with disaster ever since. The city's main Jesuit church suffered a minor indignity during the short-lived days of the Republic of Krakow when it was handed over to the Greek Orthodox Church, and the 12 apostles now doing such a fine job guarding the entrance are in fact mere copies of the 18th-century originals. Inside find a feast of delights including the remains of the famous 17th-century Father Skarga buried in the crypt. ⓐ Ul Grodzka 54 ⓣ 012 422 65 73 ⓛ 08.00–20.00

WAWEL DRAGON

Smok Wawelski was a particularly offensive dragon who allegedly lived in a cave under Wawel Hill and whose hobbies included terrorising local sheep and the occasional virgin. Naturally, a handsome young hero was dispatched to deal with the problem. Through a combination of cunning and bravado, young Krak, who just so happens to be the founder of the city, tricked Smok Wawelski into eating a sheep that had been stuffed with tar and sulphur. The result was explosive and, as they say, they all lived happily ever after. The dragon's cave, which during medieval times functioned as a rather saucy bar and brothel, is now open to the public. ⓐ Western side of Wawel Hill ⓛ 10.00–17.00 May–Nov. Admission charge

Wawel Hill & Royal Castle

The national symbol of patriotism, strength and unity for both secular and religious Poles, the breathtaking ensemble of buildings perched on top of the 50-m (164-ft) high Wawel Hill immediately south of the old town rates as a must-see attraction for anyone with even a passing interest in history. Construction of the first cathedral began soon after the founding of the bishopric of Krakow in AD 1000, with numerous additions made over the passing centuries. It was the main residence of Polish royalty from the 11th to the 17th century and the final resting place of numerous Polish kings, queens and national heroes. Highlights of the predominantly Romanesque and Gothic structures include the truly astounding cathedral and assorted rooms and chambers inside the Royal Castle or its grounds:

Cathedral Museum Opened in 1978 by Karol Wojtyla a few weeks before he became Pope John Paul II. The exhibits include some of Poland's most prized religious and royal treasures from the 13th century onwards. ☎ 012 429 33 27 🕐 09.00–16.00 Mon–Sat. Admission charge

Lost Wawel In this museum find miscellaneous objects uncovered during archaeological excavations on Wawel Hill, including parts of the first church, the Rotunda of the Virgin Mary, dating from around the 10th century. Computer-generated images show how historians and archaeologists believe the hill looked from the 10th to the 12th century. ☎ 012 422 51 55 🕐 09.30–13.00 Mon, 09.30–17.00 Tues–Fri, 11.00–18.00 Sat & Sun. Admission charge

Royal Chambers A series of beautiful and intriguing insights into life in the Polish royal court, of particular note is the extraordinary collection of tapestries commissioned by King Zygmunt August, and the Royal Audience Hall, where 194 hand-picked members from all walks of Polish life would look down on the king when he was receiving important guests or conducting trials. Note the mysterious carved wooden heads adorning the ceiling. ☎ 012 422 51 55 🕐 09.30–13.00 Mon, 09.30–17.00 Tues–Fri, 11.00–18.00 Sat & Sun. Admission charge

Treasury & Armoury Housed here are memorabilia of the Polish monarchs set inside fabulous 15th-century Gothic chambers. Among the many fine examples of arms and armour is the *Szczerbiec*, the original coronation sword. 🕐 09.30–17.00 Tues–Fri, 11.00–18.00 Sat & Sun. Admission charge

Wawel Cathedral Wawel's spectacular cathedral has been called the most important building in Poland. Inside the 14th-century walls find elaborate chapels, tombs, huge bells and great works of art. Although visually nowhere near as overwhelming as St Mary's, Wawel Cathedral wins hands down for atmosphere. If you can stomach the hordes of tourists bumping into each other and ignoring the 'no flash photography' signs, you're in for one of the highlights of the city and indeed the country. 🕐 09.00–16.00 Mon–Sat, 12.15–16.00 Sun. Admission charge

Wyspiański Museum Exhibits include Wyspiański-related temporary shows as well as a truly recommended selection of permanent displays such as his original stained-glass designs and a rather extraordinary model of Wawel after receiving the full Wyspiański treatment. ⓐ Pl Szczepański 11 ⓣ 012 422 70 21 ⓛ 10.00–18.00 Tues–Sat, 10.00–16.00 Sun. Admission charge

◆ *Wawel's spectacular cathedral*

> **PLANTY PICNIC**
> Dating from the mid-19th century, the magnificent
> 21-hectare (52-acre) park known as the Planty surrounds
> almost the entire old town. Take advantage of the city's
> army of street vendors, kebab stalls and markets, make
> yourself up a picnic and bring it here for an interesting
> and alternative lunch option.

CULTURE

Juliusz Słowacki Theatre
Built on the site of a medieval church demolished to make way
for it, the Paris Opera-inspired theatre's construction caused an
uproar among Krakow's conservative elite when it was opened in
1893. ⓐ Pl św Ducha 1 ⓣ 012 422 40 22 ⓦ www.slowacki.krakow.pl
ⓛ Opening hours vary according to performance

Palace of Art
A predominantly neo-baroque structure with art nouveau touches,
the early 20th-century Palace of Art remains one of the best
contemporary exhibition spaces in the city. ⓐ Pl Szczepańska 4
ⓣ 012 422 66 16 ⓛ 08.15–18.00 Mon–Fri, 10.00–18.00 Sat & Sun.
Admission charge

RETAIL THERAPY

A fool and his money are easily parted, especially in the
old town where prices are considerably higher than in the

rest of the city. Brimming with fancy boutiques, souvenir stalls and little else, this is a good place to browse rather than purchase.

Arkos Stuffed with goodies including holy wine, priests' robes, icons, postcards of Pope John Paul II and a feast of other Catholic treats. ⓐ Pl Mariacki 5 ⓣ 012 421 86 61 ⓛ 10.00–18.00 Mon–Fri, 10.00–14.00 Sat

Wawel Established in 1898, Wawel make their own range of chocolates, including many in fancy tins and packages that make superb gifts. ⓐ Rynek Główny 33 ⓣ 012 423 12 43 ⓦ www.wawel.com.pl ⓛ 10.00–19.00

TAKING A BREAK

U Babci Maliny £ ❶ A hugely popular country cottage-style budget Polish restaurant and one of the best places to devour plates of home-cooked *pierogi* in Krakow. Unmissable. ⓐ Ul Sławkowska 17 ⓣ 012 422 76 01 ⓛ 11.00–19.00 Mon–Fri, 12.00–19.00 Sat & Sun

Huśtawka £ ❷ Small, scruffy and full of students staring into space on broken chairs. Good bottled beer and average coffee. ⓐ Ul św Tomasza 9 ⓛ 09.00–00.00 Mon–Thur, 09.00–01.00 Fri, 10.00–01.00 Sat

Tram Bar 11 £ ❸ Old wooden tram seating and tram paraphernalia, good coffee and riotous Saturday night karaoke sessions. ⓐ Ul Stolarska 11 ⓣ 012 423 22 55 ⓛ 07.30–00.00 Mon–Fri, 11.00–00.00 Sat & Sun

U Zalipianek £ ❹ Crochet tablecloths, a hat-check granny and traditional floral designs on the walls in one of the city's most beloved communist-era leftovers. The menu includes tripe, potato pancakes and lots of herbal teas. ❹ Ul Szewska 24 ❶ 012 422 29 50 ❺ 09.00–22.00

Młyn ££ ❺ A good place to watch the world go by at the window amid a menagerie of droopy vegetables. Decent coffee and large plates of grilled meat and mush. ❹ Ul Sienna 12 ❶ 012 422 23 62 ❺ 08.00–00.00 Mon–Fri, 09.00–00.00 Sat & Sun

Noworolski ££ ❻ Gorgeous art nouveau rooms that once saw Lenin scribbling letters home to his mum, Noworolski offers coffee and cakes served by well-behaved waiters dressed as penguins. ❹ Rynek Główny 1 (Cloth Hall) ❶ 012 422 47 71 ⓦ www.noworolski.com.pl ❺ 09.00–00.00

AFTER DARK

RESTAURANTS
Zapiecek Polskie Pierogarnie £ ❼ Tiny and oh so quaint, on a good day you'll catch them making the deliciously large and ridiculously cheap *pierogi* served on plastic plates. ❹ Ul Sławkowska 32 ❶ 012 422 74 95 ⓦ www.zapiecek.eu ❺ 24 hrs

Aqua e Vino ££ ❽ Italian run and owned, the menu includes a wide range of good-looking Italian dishes, plus there's a superb wine list to complement. ❹ Ul Wiślna 5/10 ❶ 012 421 25 67 ⓦ www.aquaevino.pl ❺ 12.00–22.45

Metropolitan ££ ❾ Chess sets, supermodel waitresses and the delightful smell of bacon... Metropolitan is by far the best place in or out of the old town for breakfast any time of day. ⓐ Ul Sławkowska 3 ❶ 012 421 98 03 Ⓦ www.metropolitan-krakow.com ❸ 07.00–00.00 Mon–Sat, 07.00–22.00 Sun

Miód Malina ££ ❿ A good range of local and Italian dishes served to a clientele including loyal locals and tourists alike. Their large upmarket Polish restaurant, **Wesele** (ⓐ Rynek Główny 10), is highly recommended. ⓐ Ul Grodzka 40 ❶ 012 430 04 11 Ⓦ www.miodmalina.pl ❸ 12.00–23.00

Paese ££ ⓫ Quality Corsican cuisine on two floors. Groups out for a bit of culinary fun might like to try the excellent fondue. ⓐ Ul Poselska 24 ❶ 012 421 62 73 Ⓦ www.paese.com.pl ❸ 13.00–22.00 Mon–Thur, 13.00–23.00 Fri–Sun

● *Wierzynek has been offering fine dining for centuries*

Cyrano de Bergerac £££ 12 White tablecloths and gorgeous tapestries in a charming cellar; the French menu reads like a poem. Ⓐ Sławkowska 26 Ⓣ 012 411 72 88 Ⓦ www.cyranodebergerac.pl Ⓛ 12.00–00.00 Mon–Sat

Wierzynek £££ 13 A Polish-international restaurant that has entertained everyone from Fidel Castro to Steven Spielberg since it first opened its doors in 1364. Ⓐ Rynek Główny 15 Ⓣ 012 424 96 00 Ⓦ www.wierzynek.com.pl Ⓛ 13.00–00.00

BARS & CLUBS

Art Club Błędne Koło Everything from electro to tribal to progressive to house gets dished up inside this labyrinth of arty rooms. Ⓐ Ul Bracka 4 Ⓣ 012 431 20 52 Ⓦ www.bledne-kolo.krakow.pl Ⓛ 17.00–01.00 Mon–Wed, 17.00–05.00 Thur, 19.00–06.00 Fri & Sat

Boom Bar Rush An ear-blistering collection of corridors and a busy dance floor, full of wannabe media types and girls in cowboys hats going for it with a vengeance until sunrise. Ⓐ Ul Gołębia 6 Ⓣ 012 429 39 74 Ⓦ www.boombarrush.com Ⓛ 19.00–05.00 Tues–Sun

Cień Good-looking men in tight t-shirts pour endless waves of house music over a crowd of beautiful people high on Martini in a rather informal brick cellar atmosphere. Ⓐ Ul św Jana 15 Ⓣ 012 422 21 77 Ⓦ www.cienklub.com Ⓛ 21.00–06.00 Tues–Sat, 21.00–03.00 Sun

Cynamon Young nouveau-riche Poles sipping coffee and Peroni in the daytime and looking cool after dark on fluffy white sofas. DJs on Saturdays. ⓐ Ul św Jana 16 ⓣ 012 422 37 37 ⓛ 10.30–01.00

Irish Arms A spit and sawdust Irish pub featuring friendly staff, football on two large screens and a drunken pub quiz every Tuesday evening. ⓐ Ul Poselska 18 ⓣ 012 292 32 32 ⓛ 16.00–00.00 Mon, 12.00–00.00 Tues–Fri, 11.00–00.00 Sat & Sun

Irish Mbassy A vast pub on three floors offering everything from Playstation events to curry nights. Lads' heaven. ⓐ Ul Stolarska 3 ⓣ 012 431 02 21 ⓛ 12.00–01.00 Mon–Thur, 12.00–03.00 Fri & Sat

U Louisa Old maps and white walls in a medieval cellar, this place is something of an expat magnet thanks to the deadly combination of gorgeous barmaids and cold German lager. ⓐ Rynek Główny 13 ⓣ 012 617 02 22 ⓛ 11.00–01.00 Sun–Wed, 11.00–05.00 Thur–Sat

Nic Nowego An Irish pub with classy overtones, brimming with small-time property developers and charming locals. Come here for quality baguettes and big screen sports. ⓐ Ul św Krzyża 15 ⓣ 012 421 61 88 ⓛ 07.00–03.00 Mon–Fri, 10.00–03.00 Sat & Sun

Pauza This hidden gem is the preserve of a bunch of arty drinkers who play good music and run a small gallery showcasing young contemporary artists upstairs. ⓐ Ul Floriańska 18/3 ⓛ 10.00–00.00 Mon–Sat, 12.00–00.00 Sun

Kazimierz

The perfect antidote to the antiquated excesses of the old town, Kazimierz was established as a settlement in the 14th century to break the monopoly of the German merchants in neighbouring Krakow. The spiritual home of the city's once large Jewish community, Kazimierz's post-communist reputation as an undesirable location full of arty types was all but obliterated when Steven Spielberg chose it as one of the main locations for shooting *Schindler's List* in 1992. Now a thriving Jewish heritage tourist destination as well as the location of some of the best bars and cafés in Krakow, Kazimierz offers a beguiling mix of sights and sensations with a distinctively edgy feel that many visitors find impossible to resist.

SIGHTS & ATTRACTIONS

JEWISH KAZIMIERZ
Galicia Jewish Museum
Housed inside an old Jewish factory, this superb museum organises a range of photographic exhibitions and also has a good café and bookshop. ⓐ Ul Dajwór 18 ⓣ 012 421 68 42 ⓦ www.galiciajewishmuseum.org ⓛ 09.00–19.00. Admission charge

Isaac's Synagogue
Dating from 1644 this Judaic-baroque synagogue is still in the process of renovation. The stunning interior is a must-see. Also of interest are the old black-and-white films on show, depicting

Jewish life in Kazimierz before World War II. ⓐ Ul Kupa 18
🕐 09.00–17.00 Sun–Thur, 09.00–14.00 Sat. Admission charge

Old Synagogue

The oldest preserved synagogue in Poland, dating from what's
believed to be the early 15th century, and now a fine museum
and bookshop. ⓐ Ul Szeroka 24 ☎ 012 422 09 62 🕐 10.00–16.00
Wed–Mon, 10.00–17.00 Fri. Admission charge

⬤ The Old Synagogue, Kazimierz

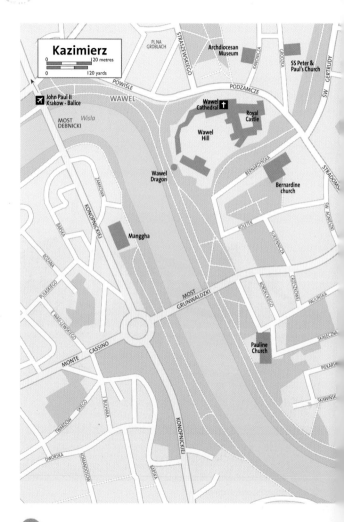

Kazimierz

0 ————— 20 metres
0 ————— 120 yards

John Paul II
Krakow - Balice

Wisła

MOST
DEBNICKI

POWISLE

WAWEL

PL. NA
GROBLACH

STRASZENSKIEGO

Archdiocesan
Museum

KANONICZA

GRODZKA

SS Peter &
Paul's Church

SW. GERTRUDY

PODZAMCZE

Wawel
Cathedral

Royal
Castle

Wawel
Hill

Wawel
Dragon

BERNARDYNSKA

Bernardine
church

STRADOMSKA

SW. AGNIESZKI

KOLETEK

SMOCZA

ZWIERZYNIECKA

KONOPNICKIEJ

BARSKA

ROZANA

Manggha

PULASKIEGO

E. WASILEWSKIEGO

MOST
GRUNWALDZKI

KONOPCZYNSKIEGO

SENACKA

CZESTOCHOWA

PALTOWSKA

SKALECZNA

Pauline
Church

PIEKARSKA

SKAWINSK

MONTE

CASSINO

TWARDOWSKIEGO

T. BULHAKA

DWORSKA

SMUGOSSON

BARSKA

KONOPNICKIEJ

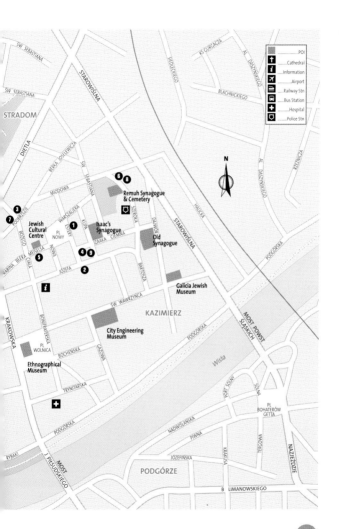

Remuh Synagogue & Cemetery

Built in 1553 and renovated in 1829, the spectacularly restored
Remuh Synagogue is the only remaining active Orthodox
synagogue in Krakow. Of Kazimierz's three remaining Jewish
cemeteries, the one here is by far the most interesting. In use
until 1800, it contains the graves of many of Krakow's most
important religious and secular Jews. Perhaps the most famous
of all the graves, of which many are of the old Jewish style
before it became fashionable for Jews to model their graves
along Christian design, is that of the 16th-century Rabbi Moses

● The Remuh Cemetery – final resting place of many of Krakow's Jews

Isserles, better known as the Remuh, and the father of the synagogue's founder. ⓐ Ul Szeroka 40 ⓣ 012 429 57 35 ⓛ 09.00–16.00 Sun–Fri. Admission charge

OTHER SIGHTS & ATTRACTIONS
City Engineering Museum
Two museums in one, this place offers a brilliant collection of old cars, trams and other motorised transport plus the rather bizarre Fun & Science exhibition. ⓐ Ul św Wawrzyńca 15 ⓣ 012 421 12 42 ⓛ 10.00–16.00 Tues–Sun. Admission charge

Ethnographical Museum
Situated inside Kazimierz's former town hall in what was once the centre of its grand market square, this often overlooked museum offers a fascinating insight into local Polish folk culture. ⓐ Pl Wolnica 1 ⓣ 012 430 55 63 ⓛ 11.00–19.00 Wed & Fri, 11.00–21.00 Thur, 11.00–15.00 Sun. Admission charge

Pauline Church
Way back in 1079 the Bishop of Krakow, Stanisław Szczepański, found himself on the wrong end of an accusation of treason from King Bolesław the Bold. The bishop was subsequently beheaded, and as so often happens in the stuff of legend the royal family fell under a curse. To appease Szczepański's spirit the family built this fine church, which, as well as having one of the best stories in Krakow as its reason for existence, is also notable for being the final resting place of our old friend Stanisław Wyspiański. ⓐ Ul Skałeczna ⓣ 012 421 74 18 ⓛ 07.00–19.00

PLAC NOWY

With the exception of the rather charming red brick rotunda at its centre dating from 1900, Plac Nowy, Kazimierz's central marketplace and modern spiritual focal point, is something of a blot on the landscape. However, as a snapshot that defines what Kazimierz was and is, there's nothing better. A microcosm of local history, Plac Nowy was until the outbreak of World War II the city's Jewish market, with the rotunda serving as the ritual slaughterhouse. Now the area has grown into something of an anomaly, with a fine daily market (see page 46), kebab stalls frequented by the local riff-raff, and a ring of bars and cafés overflowing with Krakow's moneyed bohemian 20-somethings.

CULTURE

Jewish Cultural Centre

Opened in 1993 under the auspices of the Judaica Foundation, the Jewish Cultural Centre operates out of a beautifully renovated 19th-century prayer house and offers educational programmes, lectures and other Jewish-related services to the whole community. The centre also organises the annual Bajit Chadasz (Jewish Cultural Month) every autumn. ⓐ Ul Rabina Beera Meiselsa 17 ⓣ 012 430 64 49 ⓦ www.judaica.pl ⓛ 10.00–18.00 Mon–Fri, 10.00–15.00 Sat, 10.00–14.00 Sun

RETAIL THERAPY

For information on the fabulous bric-à-brac shops and market in Kazimierz, see page 46.

High Fidelity A true labour of love courtesy of one of Kazimierz's distinctly different characters. Find among the wall-to-wall collection of rare vinyl several oddball releases from the 70s and 80s as well as the occasional communist-issue Western classic.
ⓐ Ul Podbrzezie 6 ⓣ 0506 18 44 79 ⓛ 12.00–16.00 Mon–Fri, 11.00–14.00 Sat

TAKING A BREAK

Les Couleurs £ ❶ Hot croissants and an existential-looking rabble in this French-inspired gap filler. Reminiscent of a classic Parisian bar, down to the reams of smoke and jocular bar staff.
ⓐ Ul Estery 10 ⓣ 012 429 42 70 ⓛ 07.00–00.00 Mon–Thur, 07.00–02.00 Fri, 08.00–02.00 Sat, 08.00–00.00 Sun

Kolanko Number 6 £ ❷ If you can find a better spot anywhere on the planet run by a plumber, named after a piece of plumbing pipe and containing a dentist's chair, then you certainly get about. Good music, average coffee and fine pancakes. ⓐ Ul Józefa 17
ⓣ 012 292 03 20 ⓛ 10.30–23.00

Bagelmama ££ ❸ The best bagels in Poland, and it's a fine place to visit for its relaxed atmosphere and good food including a menu of above-average Mexican dishes. ⓐ Ul Podbrzezie 2 ⓣ 012

431 19 42 Ⓦ http://bagelmama.com ⏱ 10.00–19.00 Tues–Sun

Singer ££ ❹ Refusing to fit any category at all, Singer is one of those top places that helps a newcomer feel at home and fall in love with Krakow. The unique atmosphere, bizarre sewing machine theme and all, will have you returning again and again. ⓐ Ul Estery 22 ☎ 012 292 06 22 ⏱ 09.00–03.00 Sun–Thur, 09.00–05.00 Fri & Sat

AFTER DARK

RESTAURANTS

Mleczarnia £ ❺ Like drinking on the set of Steptoe and Son with the cast of the *Rocky Horror Picture Show*, this classic Kazimierz haunt offers a great place for an afternoon pick-me-up or more lively adventures after the sun goes down. ⓐ Ul Rabina Beera Meiselsa 20 ☎ 012 421 85 32 ⏱ 10.00–02.00 Sun–Thur, 10.00–04.00 Fri & Sat

Bombaj Tandoori ££ ❻ A seemingly hastily converted Polish cafeteria. The ambience is provided by throwing a few ethnic prints on the walls, splashing out on a Best of Bollywood CD and keeping the lights down low. The Indian food stands head and shoulders above most spicy options available countrywide. ⓐ Ul Szeroka 7 ☎ 012 422 37 97 Ⓦ www.bombaj-tandoori.com.pl ⏱ 12.00–23.00 Sun–Thur, 12.00–00.00 Fri & Sat

Edo ££ ❼ Exquisitely prepared sushi and other Japanese favourites inside something that wouldn't look out of place in a Kyoto back street. Excellent value too. Put on some clean socks before booking a table in the private area. ⓐ Ul Bożego Ciała 3 ⓣ 012 422 24 24 ⓦ www.edosushi.pl ⓛ 12.00–22.00 Sun–Wed, 12.00–23.00 Thur–Sat

Klezmer Hois ££ ❽ Located inside the old Jewish bath house this veritable jumble sale of a restaurant offers fine traditional dining at its best. Even the hordes of tourists fail to rub you up the wrong way, it's that good. Live Jewish music every evening adds to the magic. ⓐ Ul Szeroka 6 ⓣ 012 411 12 45 ⓦ www.klezmer.pl ⓛ 10.00–22.00

Pepe Rosso ££ ❾ A bit of an anomaly for Kazimierz, there are neither gimmicks nor weirdos to be found here, just a highly recommended menu of Italian dishes served professionally

⬥ *Underneath the arches at Pepe Rosso*

inside either a lovely old vaulted cellar or a bright minimalist setting on the ground floor. ⓐ Ul Kupa 15 ⓣ 012 431 08 75 ⓦ www.peperosso.pl ⓛ 12.00–23.00

BARS & CLUBS

Alchemia The best thing in Krakow or a pretentious pit depending on where you stand, Alchemia is the city's unofficial headquarters of hip. Features include a self-service bar, theatre and live music performances. ⓐ Ul Estery 5 ⓣ 012 421 22 00 ⓛ 09.00–04.00 Tues–Sun, 10.00–04.00 Mon

Buena Vista Passing itself off as a restaurant (it has to be said that the Cuban menu isn't that bad, and even has a passable version of the national *moros y cristianos*), this well thought-out, slick (yet casual) affair is a fine place to sit with friends and demolish a few mojitos as part of a perfect prelude to a night on the tiles of Kazimierz. ⓐ Ul Józefa 26 ⓣ 0668 02 48 19 ⓛ 12.00–01.00 Sun–Thur, 12.00–02.00 Fri & Sat

Club Clu Choose from chic conversations on large white sofas to space-age adventures on a dance floor that plays a mixed variety of good music. ⓐ Ul Szeroka 10 ⓣ 012 429 26 09 ⓛ 18.00–01.00 Mon–Wed, 18.00–05.00 Thur–Sat

Mechanoff Green and metallic, spooky and very Polish, what is in itself a bar of note most nights of the week transforms itself on Wednesdays and Saturdays into a venue for some of the city's more outspoken and eccentric DJs. ⓐ Ul Estery 8 ⓣ 012 422 70 98 ⓛ 10.00–01.00 Mon–Thur, 10.00–02.00 Fri,

10.00–03.00 Sat, 09.00–01.00 Sun

Moment A large metallic bar, glassed-in beer garden and hundreds of clocks on the walls create a memorable backdrop for the great and the good of Kazimierz to descend to nightly for intense sessions of booze and chatter. ⓐ Ul Józefa 34 ⓣ 0668 03 40 00 ⏰ 09.00–00.00 Sun–Thur, 09.00–01.00 Fri & Sat

Opium Overflowing with young professionals who themselves are more often than not overflowing with expensive cocktails, Opium's red lighting policy ensures everybody looks like a supermodel regardless of where they were standing in the queue when the beauty was being handed out. Best of all here is the terrace. ⓐ Ul Jakuba 19, off Józefa ⓣ 012 421 94 61 ⏰ 16.00–01.00 Sun–Thur, 16.00–04.00 Fri & Sat

Propaganda A recommended wander behind the former Iron Curtain and one of the best communist-themed bars in the old communist bloc, this dark and moody drinking hole is littered with miscellaneous bygones from old radios to Lenin posters to some of the people who drink here. Expect a mixed crowd and a late night. ⓐ Ul Miodowa 20 ⓣ 012 292 04 02 ⏰ 11.00–03.00 Mon–Thur, 11.00–05.00 Fri & Sat

Le Scandale A vast array of backlit bottles mark this one out as a place where the young, beautiful and rich come to identify with the Kazimierz buzz. ⓐ Pl Nowy 9 ⓣ 012 430 68 55 ⏰ 08.00–03.00 Sun–Thur, 08.00–05.00 Fri & Sat

Further afield

Surplus to the magic on offer in the city centre are a handful of other treats. Grab a 24-hour public transport ticket (see page 55) and whisk yourself away to a number of Krakow's more distant tip-top attractions.

SIGHTS & ATTRACTIONS

NORTH
Celestat

The oddest museum in the city by a mile, Celestat celebrates the life and culture of the Krakow branch of Poland's decidedly

⬤ *Bust of Marcin Oracewicz outside the Celestat*

FURTHER AFIELD

eccentric Bractwo Kurkowe (Fowler Brotherhood). Established in medieval times, the merchant-class Fowler Brotherhood once trained the local citizens of a city to guard its walls by way of shooting a crossbow at a chicken stuck on the end of a long stick. Still in existence, the Bractwo Kurkowe dress in a lavish Oriental style and even go so far as to elect their own kings. The most precious possession a Fowler Brotherhood king possesses is his silver chicken. The Krakow silver chicken dates from 1565,

GRUNWALD MONUMENT

Celebrating the joint Polish-Lithuanian victory over the Teutonic Knights at the Battle of Grunwald on 15 July 1410, one of the defining moments in the history of the Polish nation and one of the greatest battles in medieval Europe, sculptor Antoni Wiwulski's (1877–1919) monument was unveiled in front of 160,000 people on the 500th anniversary of the battle in 1910. The original monument was destroyed by the occupying Nazis during World War II and wasn't rebuilt until 1976. Taking pride of place on his horse is the Polish King Władysław Jagiełła. At the front is his cousin Witold, a Lithuanian prince, and at either side are the Polish and Lithuanian armies. At the foot of the monument lies a dead Urlich von Jungingen, the so-called Grand Master of the Teutonic Order, whose dithering policy over Poland saw his demise at the battle and the beginning of the end for the once great Order. ⓐ Pl Matejki ⓜ Tram: 2, 4, 5, 13, 14, 19, 30, 34, 44, 71; Bus: 124, 152, 424, 502

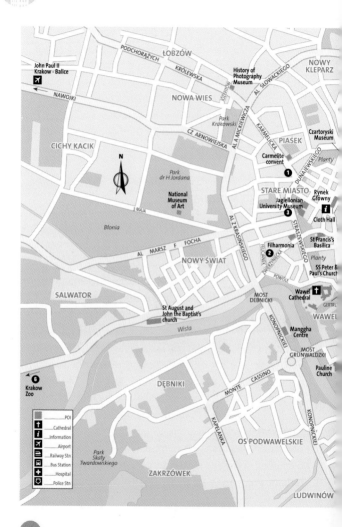

John Paul II
Krakow - Balice ✈
NAWOJKI
PODCHORĄŻYCH ŁOBZÓW
KRÓLEWSKA
History of
Photography
Museum
NOWY
KLEPARZ
AL. SŁOWACKIEGO
NOWA WIES
Park
Krakowski
CZ. ARNOWIEJSKA
AL A MICKIEWICZA
KARMELICKA
JÓZEFITÓW
DUNAJEWSKIEGO
PIASEK
Czartoryski
Museum
Planty
CICHY KACIK
Carmelite
convent ❶
Park
dr H.Jordana
National
Museum
of Art
3 MAJA
STARE MIASTO
Jagiellonian
University Museum ❸
Rynek
Główny ℹ
Cloth Hall
Błonia
AL MARSZ F FOCHA
AL Z KRAŚNIŃSKIEGO
FELICJANEK
ŚWIĘTNICKA
STRASZEWSKIEGO
Filharmonia ❷
NOWY ŚWIAT
ŚWIĘTNICKA
POWIŚLE
St Francis's
Basilica
Planty
SS Peter &
Paul's Church
SALWATOR
St August and
John the Baptist's
church
Wisła
MOST
DĘBNICKI
KONOPNICKIEJ
Wawel
Cathedral ✝
GERTRL
WAWEL
Mangha
Centre
MOST
GRUNWALDZKI
Pauline
Church
KONOPNICKIEJ
❻
Krakow
Zoo
DĘBNIKI
MONTE CASSINO
KAPELANKA
OS PODWAWELSKIE
KONOPNICKIEJ
Park
Skały
Twardowskiego
ZAKRZÓWEK
LUDWINÓW

■ ....POI
✝ ....Cathedral
ℹ ....Information
✈ ....Airport
🚉 ....Railway Stn
🚍 ....Bus Station
✚ ....Hospital
◎ ....Police Stn

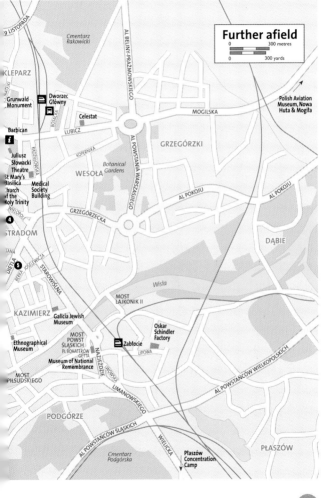

Further afield

0   300 metres

0   300 yards

9 LISTOPADA

Cmentarz Rakowicki

AL BELINY-PRAŻMOWSKIEGO

KLEPARZ

Grunwald Monument

Dworzec Główny

Celestat

MOGILSKA

Polish Aviation Museum, Nowa Huta & Mogiła

BOSACKA

RADZIŁŁOWSKA

LUBICZ

Barbican

i

GRZEGÓRZKI

KOPERNIKA

Juliusz Słowacki Theatre

WESOŁA

Botanical Gardens

AL POWSTANIA WARSZAWSKIEGO

St Mary's Basilica Church of the Holy Trinity

Medical Society Building

AL POKOJU

AL POKOJU

WIELOPOLE

GRZEGÓRZECKA

STRADOM

DĄBIE

DIETLA

BERKA JOSELEWICZA

STAROWIŚLNA

Wisła

KAZIMIERZ

MOST LAJKONIK II

Galicia Jewish Museum

Ethnographical Museum

MOST POWST ŚLĄSKICH

PL BOHATERÓW GETTA

Zabłocie

Oskar Schindler Factory

LIPOWA

NA ZJEŹDZIE

MOST PIŁSUDSKIEGO

Museum of National Remembrance

LIMANOWSKIEGO

AL POWSTAŃCÓW WIELKOPOLSKICH

PODGÓRZE

AL POWSTAŃCÓW ŚLĄSKICH

Cmentarz Podgórska

WIELICKA

PŁASZÓW

Płaszów Concentration Camp

and can be found along with a lot of other Fowler Brotherhood-related paraphernalia inside this extraordinary museum. Outside find a small bust of the Bractwo Kurkowe's most famous son, Marcin Oracewicz (see the Barbican entry on page 60), the man who shot and killed a Russian colonel with a button.

ⓐ Ul Lubicz 16 ⓣ 012 429 37 91 ⓛ 09.30–17.00 Tues–Sat
ⓝ Tram: 2, 71; Bus: 124, 152, 424. Admission charge

🔺 *Monument commemorating the medieval battle of Grunwald*

SOUTH
Fabryka Oskara Schindlera (Oskar Schindler Factory)

Born into a wealthy family in the Czech town of Svitavy, Oskar Schindler (1908–74) joined the Nazi party in 1930 and moved to Krakow soon after the German invasion of Poland in 1939, where he opened this factory. A surprisingly plain-looking building, the Fabryka Oskara Schindlera was until recently open to visitors, but at the time of writing was closed with the intention of turning the building into a museum due to open late in 2009. Such plans have been announced before and have proved fruitless; nobody is sure what exactly will happen. ⓐ Ul Lipowa 4 Ⓝ Tram: 9, 13, 32, 34; Bus: 127, 158

Manggha Centre

Almost entirely given over to the private collection of local Japanophile Feliks Jasienski's (1861–1929) Japanese artefacts, exhibits include Samurai suits, porcelain, woodcuts and some hilarious contemporary Japanese comics. ⓐ Ul Konopnickiej 26 ⓣ 012 267 27 03 Ⓛ 10.00–18.00 Tues–Sun Ⓝ Tram: 18, 19, 22; Bus: 100, 103, 112, 114, 116, 124, 128, 144, 162, 164, 169, 173, 179, 184, 194, 424. Admission charge

Museum of National Remembrance

The former site of the Apteka Pod Orłem (Pharmacy Under the Eagle), run by Tadeusz Pankiewicz, the only Gentile allowed to live inside the ghetto, and now a poignant museum portraying ghetto life with the aid of a series of moving and disturbing films and photographs. ⓐ Pl Bohaterów Getta 18 ⓣ 012 656 56 25

◆ *Oskar Schindler Factory, made famous by the Spielberg film*

🕐 10.00–14.00 Mon, 09.30–17.00 Tues–Sat 🚋 Tram: 9, 13, 32, 34; Bus: 127, 158. Admission charge

Podgórze

The fate of Krakow's sleepy southern suburb of Podgórze changed forever between 3 and 21 March 1941 when the entire Jewish population of the city was moved into a tiny part of the district

---

PŁASZÓW CONCENTRATION CAMP

Built on the site of two Jewish cemeteries in 1942, initially as a work camp for Polish, German and Jewish workers, the large and now overgrown camp at Płaszów just east of Podgórze rose to infamy soon after the arrival of the sadistic camp commandant Amon Goeth at the start of 1943, when 6,300 Krakow ghetto inhabitants were moved here. The scene of massive and brutal torture against Jews, Roma and others, there's little left to see now, except for a few monuments scattered around, including the eerie, communist-built one erected in 1964 in memory of all nationalities murdered by the Germans in the camp. To get there take tram 9, 13, 32 or 34 a couple of stops north from pl Bohaterów Getta to the Cmentarz Podgórski stop, walk up the hill and take the first right onto ul Jerozolimska. Follow the road until you reach the second camp sign and take the path to the right. The main memorials are on top of the hill to the left, just past the cave. Remember that you're walking on a mass grave site.

---

that became the Jewish ghetto. Cut off from the rest of the city by a 3-m (10-ft) high wall, some 16,000 Krakow Jews were crammed into just 320 houses and subsequently worked to death or taken to similar or worse fates at the nearby Płaszów concentration camp or the gas chambers of Auschwitz-Birkenau 80 km (50 miles) to the west. On 13 and 14 March 1943, almost two years to the day after the Nazis created it, the ghetto in Podgórze was finally liquidated. Many traces of it can still be found. There are two remaining sections of the original ghetto wall on the right-hand side of ul Lwowska as you're heading south from pl Bohaterow Getta, and another larger section to the left and behind the secondary school at ul Limanowskiego 13 a little further on.

EAST
Botanical Gardens

Founded in 1783, Poland's oldest botanical gardens offer 10 hectares (25 acres) of verdant diversions in the heart of the city. Among the usual herbaceous borders and rose gardens find several greenhouses concealing a number of surprises including a small collection of carnivorous plants. **ⓐ** Ul Kopernika 27 **ⓣ** 012 663 36 35 **ⓦ** www.ogrod.uj.edu.pl **ⓛ** 09.00–19.00 Apr–Oct **ⓝ** Tram: 2, 71; Bus: 124, 152, 424. Admission charge

Medical Society Building

Home to a fabulous Wyspiański balustrade and stained-glass windows hidden away at the back of an otherwise ordinary building dating from 1904. The stained-glass *Apollo* is particularly outstanding. Note that this isn't a museum, so you'll have to

take your chances and hope somebody's in. Knock hard and smile.
ⓐ Radziwiłłowska 4 ⓝ Tram: 2, 4, 5, 13, 14, 19, 30, 34, 71; Bus: 124, 152, 424, 502

Polish Aviation Museum

Flying machines from early wooden boneshakers to a large field of mostly Soviet-era fighter jets. The hangar behind the ticket office contains a perfectly preserved Spitfire. ⓐ Al Jana Pawła II 39 ⓣ 012 642 87 00 ⓛ 09.00–15.30 Mon, 09.00–17.00 Tues–Fri, 10.00–16.00 Sat & Sun ⓝ Tram 1, 14, 22; Bus: 609. Admission charge

WEST
History of Photography Museum

The only museum in the country given over entirely to photography is small and scruffy, but if photography is your thing then do yourself a favour and go and have a look. Among the hit-and-miss temporary exhibitions find several small rooms packed with old photographic equipment and some exceptional old black and white prints of the city. ⓐ Ul Józefitów 16 ⓣ 012 634 59 32 ⓛ 11.00–18.00 Wed–Fri, 10.00–15.30 Sat, Sun & Tues ⓝ Tram: 4, 8, 13, 14, 38; Bus: 114, 139, 159, 164, 169, 179, 192, 501. Admission charge

Krakow Zoo

As zoos go, this one is better than many in Eastern Europe, and also has the added benefit of the attached and rather fine Zoological Gardens. ⓐ Ul Kasy Oszczędności 14 ⓣ 012 425 35 51 ⓦ www.zoo-krakow.pl ⓛ 09.00–19.00 ⓝ Bus: 134 from the stop next to the park outside the National Museum of Art (see below); journey time about 20 minutes. Admission charge

National Museum of Art

One of the best museums in Poland. Along with a good collection of furniture and applied arts the museum also houses quality temporary exhibitions, and on the top floor showcases a dazzling array of Polish art from the Young Poland art movement. Highly recommended. ⓐ Al 3 Maja 1 ⓣ 012 295 55 00 ⓛ 10.00–18.00 Tues–Sat, 10.00–16.00 Sun ⓝ Tram: 5, 18; Bus: 114, 144, 164, 169, 179, 194. Admission charge

TAKING A BREAK

Coffeeheaven £ ❶ The best coffee in the city, quality sandwiches and a strict no-smoking policy. ⓐ Ul Karmelicka 8 ⓣ 012 421 30 85 ⓛ 07.00–21.30 Mon–Fri, 08.00–21.30 Sat, 09.00–21.00 Sun ⓝ Tram: 4, 8, 13, 14, 38; Bus: 601

Massolit Books & Café £ ❷ A combined bookshop and café, drop by for coffee, good books and carrot cake. ⓐ Ul Felicjanek 4 ⓣ 012 432 41 50 ⓦ www.massolit.com ⓛ 10.00–20.00 Sun–Thur, 10.00–21.00 Fri & Sat ⓝ Tram: 1, 2, 36

Rózowy Słoń £ ❸ Pink and green furniture, massive comic strips on the walls, a good-value salad bar, *pierogi* and pancakes. ⓐ Ul Straszewskiego 24 ⓣ 012 422 10 00 ⓛ 09.00–20.00 Mon–Sat, 11.00–19.00 Sun ⓝ Tram: 1, 2, 36; Bus: 103, 502

Vega ££ ❹ Feminine and terribly cutesy, this is the best place around to demolish plates of good vegetarian food and huge salads surrounded by industrial amounts of dried flowers and lace. ⓐ Ul św Gertrudy 7 ⓣ 012 422 34 94 ⓦ www.vegarestauracja.com.pl ⓛ 09.00–21.00 ⓝ Tram: 8, 10, 18, 36, 38, 40

AFTER DARK

RESTAURANTS
San Sebastian ££ ❺ Above-average nouvelle cuisine and dangerously potent cocktails. If you just need a quick snack, try their sublime pâté and toast. ⓐ Ul św Sebastiana 25 ⓣ 012 429 24 76 ⓦ www.sansebastiancafe.com ⓛ 08.00–23.00 Mon–Sat, 09.00–23.00 Sun ⓝ Tram: 19, 22; Bus: 128, 184, 603, 609

U Ziyada ££ ❻ A beguiling mix of Polish and Kurdish cooking inside a charming castle with breathtaking views of the Wisła. The setting and affordable food on offer more than make up for the long journey necessary to get here. ⓐ Ul Jodłowa 13 ⓣ 012 429 71 05 ⓦ www.uziyada.krakow.pl ⓛ 12.00–22.00 ⓝ Tram: 1, 2, 36

BARS & CLUBS
Łubu-Dubu A 70s-feel set of rooms in which to dance, drink and occasionally sit in a puddle of beer and watch a cult movie on the big screen. ⓐ Ul Wielopole 15/2 ⓣ 0694 46 14 02 ⓦ www.lubu-dubu.pl ⓛ 18.00–02.00 Sun–Tues, 18.00–03.00 Wed, 18.00–04.00 Thur, 18.00–05.00 Fri & Sat ⓝ Tram: 1, 3, 7, 13, 19, 34; Bus: 603, 609

Panorama Mediocre international food courtesy of indifferent waitresses, only worth mentioning for the spectacular view of the city from the terrace. A good spot for a summer beer, however. Find it above the Jubilat shopping centre, through an unmarked door on the right. Enter the lift and push button number 1. ⓐ Ul Zwierzyniecka 50 ⓣ 012 422 28 14 ⓛ 10.00–22.00 ⓝ Tram: 1, 2, 36; Bus: 109, 409

Plastic Lurking in a nondescript part of town close to the eastern edge of Kazimierz, Plastic offers a gay-friendly adventure with a different theme every night. The dress code is eccentric and the music policy is even madder. Fun and highly recommended. ⓐ Ul Berka Joselewicza 21C ⓣ 0691 24 07 07 ⓛ 18.00–02.00 Sun–Thur, 18.00–04.00 Fri & Sat

Qube Inside the Sheraton hotel, so the bar bill in this fine vodka joint will probably hurt more than the hangover. Over 200 vodkas and a splendid atrium setting. ⓐ Ul Powiśle 7 ⓣ 012 662 16 74 ⓦ www.sheraton.pl/krakow ⓛ 08.00–01.00 Mon–Thur, 08.00–02.00 Fri, Sat & Sun ⓝ Tram: 1, 2, 36; Bus: 109, 409

Someplace Else Gorgeous barmaids and overpriced drinks in the Sheraton's sports bar. A good place to watch football and meet some of the city's more interesting expats. ⓐ Ul Powiśle 7 ⓣ 012 662 10 00 ⓦ www.sheraton.pl/krakow ⓛ 12.00–00.00 Tues–Thur, 12.00–23.00 Sun & Mon, 12.00–01.00 Fri & Sat ⓝ Tram: 1, 2, 36; Bus: 109, 409

▶ *A bronze statue in Zakopane town centre*

Nowa Huta

On 17 May 1947 the Polish Government Presidium approved plans to construct a combined city and steelworks for 100,000 people as part of a massive project to rebuild the country at the end of World War II. The result, Nowa Huta (New Steelworks), is generally accepted to be a masterpiece of socialist realist architectural planning. Built 10 km (6 miles) east of central Krakow 'to enrage and humiliate the conservative and religious people of the city', Nowa Huta, far from becoming the socialist Utopian dream it was meant to be, turned into one of the major hotbeds of Catholic-driven anti-communist activity during the early 1980s. Slowly reinventing itself as a tourist attraction, Nowa Huta offers an intriguing adventure both as a pilgrimage site for enthusiasts of Ostalgie and, much more surprisingly, as a place to relax in the countryside and visit one or two historical religious sites.

The tourist information centre provides stacks of information on Nowa Huta but alas still only in Polish. The nice people here have designed a walking tour of the area that takes in one or two of the socialist realist sights, including the entrance to the steelworks, but concentrates mostly on the history of Kościelniki, the village that once stood here. An English translation of the route is available on the website at Ⓦ www.krakow.pl, plus it's been thoughtfully signposted in both Polish and English throughout the town. A small museum with the same opening hours featuring temporary exhibitions relating to life and culture in the area can be found inside the tourist centre building.

Tourist Information Centre ⓐ Os Słoneczne 16 ⓣ 012 643 03 03 ⓛ 10.00–14.00 Mon–Sat

⬤ *Welcome to Nowa Huta, centrepiece of the socialist realist project*

Krakow region

GETTING THERE

Trams 4 and 15 run to Nowa Huta from the city centre and take about 30 minutes to get there. Get off at the Plac Centralny stop if you want to start your adventure there, or, if you feel like seeing the main socialist realist sights the other way round, take tram 4 all the way to the Kombinat stop outside the Administrative Centre and walk back to the centre. A taxi to Nowa Huta will set you back about 20 zł.

SIGHTS & ATTRACTIONS

Arka Pana Church

Arguably the most interesting church in Krakow, the Arka Pana, or the Church of the Blessed Virgin Mary Queen of Poland (to give it its full title), was constructed with no help from the communist authorities between 1967 and 1977 to a radical design by W Pietrzyk. The estimated two million stones used for the façade were brought on site by hand, the concrete mixed in wheelbarrows, and the whole building assembled manually in the manner of a medieval cathedral. Built on a foundation that includes a stone from the tomb of St Peter in the Vatican given to the church by the late Pope John Paul II, the two-level interior is no less inspiring. Of particular note are a tiny fragment of rutile, fixed in the tabernacle and brought all the way from the moon by the crew of *Apollo 11*, a controversial figure of Christ on the cross that shows him ready to fly to heaven, and an extraordinary sculpture of Our Lady the Armoured made from 10 kg (22 lb) of shrapnel removed from Polish soldiers wounded

⬣ *Arka Pana Church, built by hand by the people of Krakow*

at Monte Cassino. The site of monthly protests against martial
law in the early 1980s, the spectacular church is about as far
removed from the average perception of Nowa Huta as it gets.
A highly recommended stop. ⓐ Pl Włosik ⏰ 06.00–19.00

Mogiła

In 1973 the boundaries of Nowa Huta changed, incorporating
a number of areas of historical interest. Particularly remarkable
is the small area known as Mogiła immediately east of the centre,
which boasts two fine churches. The first, the Assumption
of the Virgin Mary and St Wenceslas' Church, dates from the
transition period between Romanesque and Gothic styles, is
decorated with some wonderful folk paintings, and is considered
to be one of the most important religious buildings in Małopolska.
Across the street is Krakow's only wooden church. Built in 1466,
the tiny St Bartholomew's is, unusually for Poland, built in the
shape of a cross and is the only wooden church in Poland with
three naves in a hall arrangement. Ⓝ Tram: 15 or 10 from
pl Centralny east to the Klasztorna stop and head south
down Klasztorna.

Museum of the Armed Act

An intriguing museum dedicated to the people of Nowa Huta
who fought and died for their country during World War II. In
Polish only, the exhibits will be lost on most, but a visit is highly
recommended if not least for the extraordinary and disturbing
tableaux of scenes from life in Krakow between 1939 and 1945.
ⓐ Os Górali 23 ☎ 012 644 35 17 ⏰ 10.00–16.00 Tues–Sat.
Admission by donation

◔ St Bartholomew's in Mogiła sits in contrast to the concrete of Nowa Huta

Socialist realist architecture

Socialist realism was the only officially recognised art form within the Soviet Union from the 1930s until its final collapse in 1991. Supposedly capable of furthering the goals of communism, socialist realist art embodied everything from painting to architecture. More often than not a dismal attempt at elevating the working classes into heroes through a stifling collective creative process, social realism was exported on a global scale. Of the many socialist realist sights to see in Nowa Huta, the area stretching northeast from pl Centralny to the former Lenin steelworks is of most interest. The pompous and absurd Stalinist-baroque pl Centralny (Central Square) dates from 1949, has been renamed in honour of Ronald Reagan, and is currently awaiting a statue of Elvis Presley. Surrounded on three sides by large grey blocks that have received the full socialist realist treatment, five grand avenues radiate from the square, of which the partially pedestrianised al Róz to the north, where the town's statue of Lenin once stood, is perhaps the most exemplary. Along al Róz on the right is Park Ratuszowy, which, as well as offering a brief respite from the horrors of concrete, is a popular summer haunt for retired male steelworkers to sit and play cards, and gives an indication of the way the town's architects tried to blend nature, architecture and people together. A little further up, just past the tourist information centre and museum, head east on ul S Żeromskiego and follow the road round to the right and onto the huge al Solidarności (Solidarity Avenue). This brief walk takes you through a short section of leafy streets indicative of the entire town's original philosophy. Going east along al Solidarności you pass the large lake known as Zalew nad Dłubia, the site of a big water park built as part of Nowa Huta's new, friendlier image. Immediately behind the lake is the modern Santorini hotel and restaurant (see page 115), the latter of which is a good place to stop for something substantial to eat. Nowa Huta's architectural jewel in the crown can be found at the far eastern end of al Solidarności. The administrative centre of the Huta im Sendzimira (Sendzimir Steelworks Factory) is made up of two huge buildings that are generally believed to be Poland's best examples (after Warsaw's Palace of Culture and Science) of socialist realist architecture. Topped with all manner of baroque swirls and fiddly details, these ghastly beasts are referred to by the locals as the Doge, after the grand palace in Venice which they apparently resemble.

CULTURE

Ludowy Theatre

Situated between two football fields, where gangs of punks and skinheads hang around, the renowned Ludowy (People's) Theatre is famous for bringing these two warring factions together to stage a version of *Romeo and Juliet*. With its absurd Doric columns and chandeliers, a visit to the Ludowy Theatre is worth the effort, even if you're not planning to attend a performance. ⓐ Os Teatralne 34 ⓣ 012 680 21 00 ⓦ www.ludowy.pl ⓛ Opening hours vary according to production

Norwid Cultural Centre

An unremarkable building were it not for the fact that at the

top of the stairs hangs a permanent display of paintings by the famous Krakow Group. Well worth a look inside. ⓐ Os Górali 5 ⓣ 012 644 27 65 ⓦ www.okn.edu.pl ⓛ 08.00–21.00 Mon–Fri, 09.00–21.00 Sat & Sun

RETAIL THERAPY

Not unlike eating in Nowa Huta (see below), shopping in the town is a cheerless event aimed almost exclusively at the local residents. An interesting way of combining the two and making the most of a bad lot is by visiting the local outdoor market. A typical affair, as found throughout Eastern Europe, the market in Nowa Huta consists almost entirely of fake designer clothing, bin liners and food. The food, however, is represented by a good choice of fresh bread, cheese, sausages, fruit and vegetables, creating the perfect opportunity to make up a picnic that can be eaten in the park.

Nowa Huta Market ⓐ Bieńczycki Plac Targowy ⓣ 012 641 48 77 ⓛ 06.00–18.00 Mon–Fri, 06.00–14.00 Sat & Sun

TAKING A BREAK

Café Lura £ Inside the Ludowy Theatre. You'll hardly be writing postcards home about how great the place is, but it's not that bad either. It's a good stop for filling up on coffee and sticky buns before heading off on your next socialist realist adventure. ⓐ Os Teatralne 34 ⓣ 012 680 21 26 ⓛ One hour before and 30 minutes after performances

Cocktail Bar £ Multicoloured walls, cheap burgers, beer and average coffee. This is the Nowa Huta experience at its best. ⓐ Os Centrum C ⓣ 012 644 28 07 ⓛ 10.00–23.00 Mon–Fri, 11.00–23.00 Sat & Sun

AFTER DARK

Santorini ££ If it's after dark and you're in Nowa Huta then you're probably staying in this hotel (below) anyway. Featuring nice modern touches and English-speaking waiters, this is by far the best restaurant in Nowa Huta, but it's recommended you avoid the international dishes and go for something Polish. ⓐ Ul Bulwarowa 35B ⓣ 012 644 91 11 ⓛ 10.00–22.00

ACCOMMODATION

Santorini ££ Good-value 3-star accommodation in a large pink building immediately west of the Zalew nad Dłubia lake. Facilities include satellite television, minibars and internet access. ⓐ Ul Bulwarowa 35B ⓣ 012 680 51 95 ⓦ www.santorini.krakow.pl

Zakopane

Poland's biggest fire hazard, the fabulous wooden town of Zakopane has been attracting hikers, artists and winter sports enthusiasts since Tytus Chałubinski announced the beneficial healing properties of its climate to an unsuspecting world in 1886. Nestled inside a small valley between the jagged Tatra Mountains and the little hillside hamlet of Gubałówka 110 km (68 miles) south of Krakow, the country's unofficial winter capital, with its trademark Zakopane Style timber houses, fine skiing and fresh mountain air, offers an enticing diversion away from its mighty neighbour in the north.

Not including the mountains, Zakopane can be roughly dissected into three main areas. The compact town centre is the first natural port of call, and is the scene of the town's main action as well as where the major sights are to be found. To the north is Gubałówka, a tiny settlement on top of a hill reached by a funicular railway; there's lots to do there and it's a good place to enjoy local food and a spectacular view of the Tatras. Finally there's the skiing, which in town is pretty tame and can be found in several places around the edge of Zakopane. The serious skiing is further south and is accessed via a cable-car ride from the south of the town. Buying a map before you travel to Zakopane is recommended. The Empik bookshop (see page 137) stocks several.

Not surprisingly for a major tourist destination, Zakopane is brimming with private tourist information centres, all of which offer the same basic services and sell a few maps and small guides to the town and surrounding mountains. The official, state-owned tourist point sells maps and local guidebooks and

▲ *The rugged Tatras rise over Zakopane*

● *Detail from St Mary's Cemetery*

provides a few free brochures in English. Still relying on Polish tourists for most of its trade, Zakopane is yet to offer anywhere near the kind of English-language services you get in Krakow.

Tourist Information Centre ⓐ Ul Kościuszki 17 ⓣ 018 201 22 11
ⓦ www.zakopane.pl ⓛ 09.00–17.00 Mon–Fri

GETTING THERE

By road

A regular bus service runs daily between 05.10 and 21.05 from Krakow's main bus station, taking about two hours in good weather. A one-way ticket costs 15 zł and can be bought from the driver. Depending on whether you catch a state-run or privately operated bus, you'll be dropped off either at the central bus station (with the former) or outside the Grand Hotel. Either way, the town centre is a five-minute walk west along ul Kościuszki. The bus station is a lacklustre affair, useful for its toilet facilities (1.50–2 zł) and a small shop in the main building (ⓛ 08.00–19.00) that also functions as the left luggage office (5 zł per piece). There's an ATM outside. Taxis should be parked outside the station and will set you back about 5 zł for a ride into the town centre. Alternatively, go into the Grand Hotel a few metres west of the station and ask them to call you one.

By rail

With the likelihood of a long journey on an ancient train with no facilities and the distinct possibility of having to change trains at least once along the way, travelling by rail to Zakopane is not recommended. Zakopane's train station is next to the bus

station and is even less glamorous. The only advantage of leaving bags here is that there are a number of lockers (4–8 zł), which can be accessed around the clock. Getting into town is the same as if you're arriving by bus.

SIGHTS & ATTRACTIONS

St Mary of Częstochowa Church

Built between 1847 and 1851 by Sebastian Gasienica Sobczak, St Mary's is the oldest wooden church in Zakopane. The graveyard to the right is the final resting place of many of the town's most famous sons and daughters. ⓐ Ul Kościeliska 4 ⓛ 06.30–19.30

Tatra Museum

A fitting dedication to Zakopane's founding father Tytus Chałubinski (1820–99), this serves as a good introduction to the life and culture of the local *górale* mountain folk as well as the flora and fauna of the region. Not much in English, however. ⓐ Ul Krupówki 10 ⓣ 018 201 52 05 ⓛ 09.00–17.00 Tues–Sat, 09.00–15.00 Sun. Admission charge

Torture Museum

Two small and rather macabre rooms above the Morskie Oko restaurant, including iron maidens, racks and other gruesome devices. ⓐ Ul Krupówki 30 ⓣ 018 201 50 66 ⓛ 10.00–20.00. Admission charge

Zakopane Style Museum

Housed inside the charming Willa Koliba (1894), this was the

⏺ *Unusual folk art, Tatra Museum*

first house to be designed and built in the distinctive Zakopane Style by local resident and minor celebrity Stanisław Witkiewicz. Here you'll find a fairytale recreation of how people used to live in the region at the turn of the 20th century. ⓐ Ul Kościeliska 18 ⓘ 018 201 36 02 ⓛ 09.00–17.00 Wed–Sat, 09.00–15.00 Sun. Admission charge

THE TATRAS

A magnificent chain of peaks straddling Poland and Slovakia, the Tatras (or the High Tatras to give them their proper name) form the highest section of the Carpathians. With peaks in Poland rising to almost 2,500 m (8,202 ft), the Polish Tatras are a truly wonderful sight, featuring dense forests full of brown bears, eagles, chamois and other forgotten creatures, plus large lakes and an abundance of mountain huts available for rent. A popular summertime hiking, rock climbing and paragliding destination, the Tatras really come to life during the winter, when the Poles turn out in droves to take advantage of the good skiing, snowboarding and snowmobile adventures the mountains have to offer.

The **Tatra National Park Museum** is an indication that the West is yet to discover the Tatras – it's sadly lacking in English explanations – but it's a good place to pick up information on things to see and do in the mountains. ⓐ Ul Chałubińskiego 42A ⓘ 018 206 32 03 ⓛ 08.00–15.00 Mon–Sat

RETAIL THERAPY

If you like cheap souvenirs you'll love Zakopane. Completely obscuring the fabulous architecture in the town centre, the temptation to buy a fake rug or hand-carved wooden spoon from one of the endless rows of identical market stalls is hard to resist. The best place to pick up a memento of your visit is in the large market at the northern end of ul Krupówki. This is also the best place in town to pick up CDs of the local folk music, which ranges in style from the sublime to the unpalatable.

Foto Koliba A good supply of disposable cameras plus accessories for digital and analogue cameras of every persuasion. ⓐ Ul Krupówki 17 ☎ 018 201 19 92 ⏱ 09.00–21.00

Galeria M Jędrysiak A small gallery and shop at the southern entrance to the market on ul Krupówki. Some quality paintings and sculptures by artists from all over the country. ⓐ Ul Droga na Gubałówkę 2 ☎ 018 201 35 46 ⏱ 12.00–17.00

TAKING A BREAK

Almost every menu in town features a few *górale*-style, meat-heavy dishes, guaranteed to keep you at bursting point for several hours. In summer the streets offer countless opportunities to eat on the hoof, with fabulous grilled meat being sold every few metres and ladies everywhere selling *precel* and *oscypek*.

Gubałówka £ A large mountain lodge with breathtaking views of the mountains in the little settlement of the same name at the top of Zakopane's fun funicular ride, the only thing missing here is Julie Andrews. Young girls in traditional costumes bring good-value mountain food to your table while you dream about giving up the rat race and farming goats for the rest of your days. ⓐ Ul Gubałówka ⓣ 018 206 36 30 ⓛ 10.00–18.00

Morskie Oko £ A curious combination of mountain hut and canteen, complete with a grand piano and retirement-age dinner ladies. Average quality *żurek* and *bigos* dished out before your very eyes. Excellent if you're in a hurry, and not too bad if you're not. ⓐ Ul Krupówki 30 ⓣ 018 201 50 66 ⓛ 08.00–22.00

Grand Hotel Bar £££ Rocket-fuel espressos in the comfort of a posh hotel bar, plus food from the adjoining restaurant brought to your table if you're feeling peckish. Hardly indicative of Zakopane, but who cares? The private buses back to Krakow leave from right outside the window, making this place possibly the best waiting room in Poland. ⓐ Ul Gościuszki 19 ⓣ 018 202 45 10 ⓛ 13.00–00.00

AFTER DARK

RESTAURANTS
Gazdowo Kuźnia ££ Sit inside and eat your mountain food or scrambled eggs and bacon while reclining in a sleigh, or if it's

summer have one of their kebabs from the stall outside. The kebab meat in question is carved straight off a rotating pig, slipped inside a piece of hot crispy bread and garnished with salad and hot chilli mayonnaise. This alone is worth the trip to Zakopane. ⓐ Ul Krupówki 1 ⓣ 018 201 72 01 ⓛ 10.00–23.00

BARS

Paparazzi A Polish institution, the Paparazzi chain's Zakopane outlet features the usual walls lined with iconic photographs as well as a range of quality cocktails to keep you in here until well after throwing-out time. ⓐ Ul Gen Galicy 8 ⓣ 018 206 32 51 ⓛ 16.00–01.00 Mon–Fri, 12.00–01.00 Sat & Sun

Piano Café Zakopane's quirkiest drinking establishment features glass-topped tables full of plants, the usual array of wooden seating and, strangely, some swings by the bar. ⓐ Ul Krupówki 63 ⓛ 15.00–00.00

ACCOMMODATION

A town of just 30,000, Zakopane receives around 1.5 million tourists every year. Accordingly, accommodation books up well in advance, especially during the peak winter season between Christmas and the start of March. The tourist information centre can help you find a bed, or, depending on the condition of your wallet, try one of the two following options.

Gospoda Pod Niebem £ A dirt-cheap Gubałówka accommodation option inside a lovely wooden house. The basic but charming

rooms come with simple showers and not a lot else, but the views are spectacular if you choose the right room. Ul Droga Stanisława Zubka 5 018 206 29 09 www.podniebem.zakopane.pl

Grand Hotel Stamary £££ Catering to the local nouveau riche, this magnificent hotel next to the bus station offers quality rooms and top-notch service for the price of a Travelodge in Northampton. Other incentives for sleeping here include a fully equipped spa and wellness centre. Ul Gościuszki 19 018 202 45 10 www.stamary.pl

Jewish figures for sale, Kazimierz

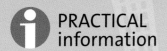

PRACTICAL information

Directory

GETTING THERE

By air

Krakow is served by direct flights from most major airports in Europe. Several low-cost airlines as well as the Polish national carrier, LOT, and British Airways operate direct daily flights from a number of airports in the UK. Flying time from London is about two and a half hours.

Krakow Balice Airport ⓐ Ul Kapitana Medweckiego 1

ⓣ 012 639 30 00 ⓦ www.lotnisko-balice.pl

British Airways ⓦ www.britishairways.com

easyJet ⓦ www.easyjet.com

LOT ⓦ www.lot.pl

Ryanair ⓦ www.ryanair.com

Many people are aware that air travel emits CO_2, which contributes to climate change. You may be interested in the possibility of lessening the environmental impact of your flight through the charity **Climate Care** (ⓦ www.climatecare.org), which offsets your CO_2 by funding environmental projects around the world.

By road

Before you set off in your car, be warned: Polish road fatality figures are among the worst in Europe, a result of the notoriously treacherous state of Polish roads, and the icy and snowy conditions during the winter. The bad condition of the roads in and around Krakow is being addressed, however, which will make driving a much more pleasurable thing to do.

ENTRY FORMALITIES

Poland joined the Schengen system in December 2007. Arriving in the country has never been easier, although spot passport checks are still occasionally held on the land borders. Getting in and out of Belarus, Kaliningrad and Ukraine, especially the former, still remains problematic.

Citizens from EU countries and people from Australia, New Zealand, Canada and the United States can enter Poland without a visa and stay for a period of up to three months within any one year (six months for UK passport holders). Poland's entry into the European Union was meant to simplify duty-free allowances, but there remains an enormous amount of confusion over this issue; travellers are advised to contact their local Polish embassy or consulate before they leave home.

TRAVEL INSURANCE

It's advisable to take out adequate travel insurance covering medical expenses, theft, loss, repatriation, personal liability and cancellation. EU citizens with a European Health Insurance Card (see 'Health, safety & crime', page 130) are still advised to have private medical insurance as well. If you're bringing your own vehicle ensure that you have the appropriate insurance, and remember to pack the insurance documents and your driving licence. You'll need to make a police report for non-medical claims, and ensure you keep any receipts for medical treatment.

MONEY

The Polish currency is the złoty (zł), divided into 100 groszy. Exchange bureaux (*kantor*) are common and ATMs are a standard fixture throughout Krakow. Paying by credit card is getting easier, although there are a few places in the centre that only take cash. Many places in Nowa Huta and Zakopane are yet to switch on to the pleasures of plastic. Poland plans to join the euro in 2011 (see page 17).

HEALTH, SAFETY & CRIME

Local tap water tastes funny but is safe to drink. There's little danger of getting food poisoning while in Krakow, although you should exercise caution when eating mushrooms; picking wild ones in the autumn is very much a national pastime, and Polish immune systems have built up a natural resistance to many fungi that might just lose you a night's sleep if you have a particularly sensitive stomach.

Healthcare standards remain somewhat low. Quality healthcare comes with an almost Western price-tag. All hospitals and clinics will have at least one English-speaking member of staff on duty at all times. Many chemists speak at least a little English. For more information see 'Medical services' (page 138). UK and EU citizens are entitled to reduced-cost, sometimes free, medical treatment on presentation of a valid **European Health Insurance Card** (EHIC, apply online at Ⓦ www.dh.gov.uk/travellers). On top of this, private medical insurance is still advised, and is essential for all non-EU visitors.

Krakow is a relatively safe city by European standards. The average Polish criminal is personified by the stereotypical image of the petty thief, who gets his kicks from preying on idiot foreigners who leave their wallets and mobile phones in unattended pockets.

OPENING HOURS

Most museums open at around 10.00, closing between 14.00 and early evening. Monday is the traditional day for most museums to bolt their doors. Churches generally open early to allow people to pray on the way to work. Office hours follow the same pattern as the rest of Europe, and are still often punctuated with longer-than-average lunch breaks. Banks open at around 08.00 and will stay open until 18.00 in most cases, with the majority closed on weekends. Retail hours are harder to pin down, with markets opening up around the same time you're being poured into a taxi after a night out, and other shops following from about 09.00 onwards.

TOILETS

Polish toilets, often marked with a circle for women and a triangle for men, are improving, but many leave much to be desired. Several places, including decent restaurants, bus and train stations, and McDonald's (for non-customers), charge a small fee for using their toilets, usually 1.50–2 zł. Public toilets simply don't exist, but Galeria Kazimierz and Galeria Krakowska (see pages 24 & 26) have free toilet facilities.

CHILDREN

Poland is a child-friendly society that somehow manages to overlook the basic needs of children. Although there are plenty of parks and adventure playgrounds scattered around Krakow, finding baby-changing facilities, more than one high chair or a glass smaller than a bucket in most restaurants remains a fruitless task. As well as the zoo (see page 99) and water park at Nowa Huta, parents might like to wind their children down a little at the **H Jordana Park** (ⓐ Al 3 Maja 11 ⓝ Tram: 15, 18), which has an excellent playground as well as rowing boats and a few other things to keep the little ones occupied.

COMMUNICATIONS

Internet

Garinet Tucked away at the back of a narrow alleyway, find a handful of fast machines complete with Skype, plus the option of cheap international calls courtesy of a standard telephone. ⓐ Ul Floriańska 18 🕐 09.00–00.00

Koffeina A proper internet café with good coffee, USB sockets, printing and cheap international telephone calls. ⓐ Rynek Główny 23 ☎ 012 432 94 94 🕐 24 hrs

Phones

Payphones are expensive and cards are often sold in Krakow without any credit on them. Your best option is to use one of the VOIP services available in many internet cafés (see above) or a local SIM card. If you've got an unblocked mobile phone and you are too cheap to roam, take advantage of one of Poland's

TELEPHONING POLAND

To call Krakow from abroad, dial your international access code (usually 00), then the national code for Poland (48), followed by the area code for Krakow minus the initial 0 (12) and the local number. Somewhat confusingly, the prefix 012 at the start of a telephone number is both the code for Krakow and a part of the number. So, if you're calling from one Krakow landline to another you'll need to include the 012 at the beginning. Likewise, if you're calling Krakow from another city in Poland, dial the 10-figure number starting with 012. If you're calling a landline from a Polish mobile, just dial the 10-figure number. If you're using the Plus GSM service, drop the first 0.

TELEPHONING ABROAD

To phone home from Krakow, dial the outgoing code (00), followed by the relevant country code (see below), area code (minus the initial 0 if there is one) and local number.

Australia 43
New Zealand 64
Republic of Ireland 353
South Africa 27
UK 44
USA & Canada 1

National enquiries ⓘ 912
International operator ⓘ 901

three mobile operators' prepaid services. All three companies sell SIM starters packs for less than 10zł. These can be bought from the individual mobile operator outlets throughout the city (see below), in most kiosks and at the airport, train and bus stations.

Era ⓐ Ul Wielicka 259 (Tesco) ☎ 012 657 78 98 🕒 09.00–21.00 Mon–Sat, 09.00–19.00 Sun

Orange ⓐ Ul Podgórska 34 ☎ 012 433 10 90 🕒 10.00–22.00 Mon–Sat, 10.00–20.00 Sun

Plus GSM ⓐ Ul Królewska 57 ☎ 012 396 21 50 🕒 10.00–19.00 Mon–Fri, 10.00–14.00 Sat

Post

The Polish postal service is reliable albeit a little slow at times, with letters and postcards often taking a week or more to reach the UK. Krakow is not short on post offices or boxes, the latter being red with a yellow post horn on a blue background. The city's main post office (see below) uses a queue ticket system for everything except sending parcels (at windows 1–4) and buying stamps (windows 2–14). Letters and postcards cost 1.30 zł to send within Poland and 2.40 zł to all other destinations.

Main Post Office (Poczta Główna) ⓐ Ul Westerplatte 20 ☎ 012 422 66 96 🕒 07.30–20.30 Mon–Fri, 08.00–14.00 Sat, 09.00–14.00 Sun

ELECTRICITY

Polish domestic electricity flows out of the walls at 220 V, 50 Hz, and sockets are of the round, two-pin European variety. People travelling from outside continental Europe should bring an appropriate adaptor, and US travellers will need a transformer as well.

TRAVELLERS WITH DISABILITIES

Facilities for the disabled are only just starting to appear,
mostly due to the fact that EU legislation demands it. New
buildings must meet rigid standards, but since one of the
main reasons for visiting Krakow is to have a poke around
its antiquated sights, this is little comfort. The Poles are often
their own worst enemies and are in such a general state of
denial over these issues that welcome additions to the city, like
disabled parking spaces that the able-bodied masses consider
fair game, might as well not exist at all. Getting around isn't
a lot better, although all of the new bendy buses in town are
equipped with disabled access as standard. To date, only tram
lines 8, 34, 36 and 38 are capable of accommodating wheelchairs.
The following may be of some use:

Disabled Persons Transport Advisory Committee UK
Ⓦ www.dptac.gov.uk/door-to-door

Trip Scope UK Ⓣ 0845 758 641 Ⓦ www.tripscope.org.uk

SATH (Society for Accessible Travel & Hospitality) US
ⓐ 347 Fifth Ave, Suite 610, New York, NY 10016 Ⓣ 212 447 7284
Ⓕ 212 725 8253 Ⓦ www.sath.org

TOURIST INFORMATION

The city centre is teeming with tourist information centres, both
state-run and private, offering information, leaflets, guided tours
and much more. Remember, however, that advice isn't always
impartial. Working for a small cash commission is an accepted
way for tourist information staff to top up a modest salary. The
city's official tourism website is Ⓦ www.krakow.pl, and two good
ports of call are:

○ *Sights in the city centre are well signposted*

Małopolska Tourist Information Inside the Cloth Hall. ⓐ Rynek
Główny 1/3 ⓣ 012 421 77 06 ⓛ 09.00–17.00
Tourist Information Office State-run, and quite possibly the best
in town. ⓐ Pl Mariacki 3 ⓣ 012 431 16 78 ⓛ 09.00–18.00 Mon–Sat,
09.00–15.00 Sun

BACKGROUND READING

Three books worth picking up are all produced by the local
publisher Wydawnictwo Bezdroża. Written by locals with a
passion for the areas they cover, each one contains heaps of
valuable insights into (and strange stories behind) the people,

buildings and events that have shaped the city. Individual guidebooks in their own right, complete with walking tours, information on bars and restaurants and some great colour photography, the series also provides the necessary background reading that the vast majority of other locally published books overlook. Sadly lacking in detail in just one or two areas, the well-translated, pocket-size books cost around 35 zł each in the Empik Megastore (see below).

Krakow's Kazimierz by Agnieszka Legutko-Ołownia. A brilliant evocation of Krakow's former Jewish quarter and rapidly up-and-coming bohemian district. Essential reading for anyone with a special interest in Kazimierz.

Krakow's Nowa Huta by Maciej Miezian. The first book in English to break away from the obsession with Nowa Huta's communist past. Pages and pages of magnificent and often hilarious insights, with tours of the hitherto unpublished rural parts of Nowa Huta.

Krakow's Old Town by Maciej Miezian. Verging on a masterpiece, covering everything you ever wanted to know about the old town and Wawel. Old-town sights as well as stories about alchemists, butchers and a very faithful dog called Dżok (Jock).

Empik Megastore Along with the above-mentioned books, Empik's flagship Krakow store stocks a huge selection of CDs, DVDs, maps, guidebooks and some English-language paperbacks. ⓐ Rynek Główny 5 ⓣ 012 429 67 23 ⓒ 09.00–22.00

Emergencies

EMERGENCY NUMBERS

Ambulance ☎ 999
Fire ☎ 998
Police ☎ 997

It's unlikely anyone at the other end of the three numbers listed above will speak English. However, the Polish police now operate a daytime and evening emergency call centre for foreigners in English and German that closes around the time you'll probably need it (🕐 08.00–00.00): from a local landline, call ☎ 0800 20 03 00 and if roaming call ☎ +48 22 601 55 55.

MEDICAL SERVICES

Krakowskie Pogotowie Ratunkowe (Krakow Emergency Ambulance Service) English-speaking medical services for emergencies. ⓐ Ul Łazarza 14 ☎ 999 (from a fixed line telephone) ☎ 112 (from a mobile phone) 🕐 24 hrs

Chemist
Apteka ⓐ Ul Kalwaryjska 94 ☎ 012 656 18 50 🕐 24 hrs

Dentists
Denta-Med ⓐ Ul Austiańska 13 ☎ 012 292 33 00 🕐 24 hrs
Dent America ⓐ Pl Szczepański 3 ☎ 012 421 89 48
ⓦ www.dentamerica.pl 🕐 09.00–20.00 Mon–Fri, 09.00–14.00 Sat

EMERGENCY PHRASES

Help!	**Fire!**	**Stop!**
Pomocy!	Pożar!	Stop!
Po-mo-ste!	*Po-jar!*	*Stop!*

Call an ambulance/a doctor/the police/the fire service!
Wezwać pogotowie/lekarza/policję/straż pożarna!
*Ve-zvach po-go-toh-vyeh/le-ka-jah/po-lee-tsyeh/
straj po-jar-nom!*

POLICE
Old Town Central Police Station @ Rynek Główny 29
☏ 012 61 57 319

EMBASSIES
Australia @ Ul Nowogrodzka 11, Warsaw ☏ 022 521 34 44
Canada @ Ul Matejki 1/5, Warsaw ☏ 022 584 31 00
New Zealand @ Al Ujazdowskie 51, Warsaw ☏ 022 521 05 00
Republic of Ireland @ Ul Mysia 5, Warsaw ☏ 022 849 66 33
South Africa @ Ul Koszykowa 54, Warsaw ☏ 022 625 62 28
UK @ Al Róż 1, Warsaw ☏ 022 311 00 00
USA @ Al Ujazdowskie 29/31, Warsaw ☏ 022 625 14 01

A

accommodation 37–41
Nowa Huta 115
Zakopane 125–6
air travel 50, 128
alcohol 24, 29
aquarium 48
Archaeology Museum 48
Archdiocesan Museum 60
architecture 104, 112–13
Arka Pana Church 108–10
arts see culture
Assumption of the Virgin
Mary & St Wenceslas'
Church 110

B

background reading 136
Barbican 60–1
bars, clubs & pubs
see nightlife
Botanical Gardens 98
Bractwo Kurkowe 90–4
bread 27–8
Burgher Museum 64
bus travel 51, 119

C

cafés
Further afield 100–1
Kazimierz 85–6
Nowa Huta 114–15
Old town & Wawel 73–4
Zakopane 123–4
car hire 58

Cathedral 69, 70
Cathedral Museum 69
Catholicism 18
Celestat 90–94
children 132
cinema 24–6, 33
City Engineering
Museum 83
Cloth Hall 64
concessions 46
crime 131
culture 14–15, 20–2, 46
customs & duty 129–30
cycling 34
Czartoryski Museum 64–5

D

disabilities 135
driving 58, 128

E

electricity 134
embassies 139
emergencies 138–9
entertainment 31–3
see also nightlife
Ethnographical
Museum 83
events 10–15
extreme sports 34

F

Fabryka Oskara
Schindlera 95
festivals 10–15
food & drink 27–30, 130

football 34
Fowler Brotherhood 90–4

G

Galicia Jewish Museum 78
golf 36
Grunwald Monument 91
Gubałowka 116

H

H Jordana Park 132
health 130, 138
Hippolit House 64
Historical Museum
of Krakow 65
history 16–17, 91, 97
History of Photography
Museum 99
hotels
see accommodation
Huta im Sendzimira 113

I

insurance 129, 130
internet 132
Isaac's Synagogue 78–9

J

Jagiellonian University
Museum 65
Jewish Cultural Centre 84
Jewish Festival
of Culture 14–15
Jewish Krakow 14–15,
78–3, 84, 95–8
John Paul II 17, 18, 60
Juliusz Słowacki Theatre 72

K

Kazimierz 46–7, 78–89
Krakow Aquarium 48
Krakow card 46
Krakow Zoo 99–100

L

language 26, 30, 55, 139
Leonardo da Vinci 64–5
lifestyle 18–19
listings 10, 31
Lost Wawel 69
Ludowy Theatre 113

M

malls 24–6
Manggha Centre 95
markets 24, 47, 64, 84, 114, 123
Medical Society Building 98–9
Mogiła 110
money 130
Museum of the Armed Act 110
Museum of National Remembrance 95–7
music 20, 31–3
National Museum of Art 100
nightlife 31–3
    Further afield 101–2
    Kazimierz 88–9
    Nowa Huta 115
    Old town & Wawel 76–7
    Zakopane 125

Norwid Cultural Centre 113–14
Nowa Huta 104–15

O

Old Synagogue 79
Old town 60–77
opening hours 131
Oracewicz, Marcin 61
Oskar Schindler Factory 95

P

Palace of Art 72
Park Ratuszowy 112
parks & green spaces 72, 98, 99–100, 112, 122, 132
passports & visas 129
Pauline Church 83
Pharmacy Museum 49
phones 132–4
picnics 27, 72
pierogi 12, 27
Plac Nowy 84
Planty 72
Płaszów concentration camp 97
Podgórze 97–8
police 138, 139
Polish Aviation Museum 99
Pope John Paul II 17, 18, 60
post 134
public holidays 13
public transport 50–1, 54–7, 108, 119–20

R

rail travel 50–1, 119–20
Remuh Synagogue & Cemetery 82–3
restaurants 27, 29
    Further afield 101
    Kazimierz 86–8
    Old town & Wawel 74–6
    Zakopane 124–5
Royal Castle 69–70
Royal Chambers 70
Rynek Główny 65–6

S

safety 51, 130, 138–9
St Bartholomew's Church 110
St Francis's Basilica 66
St Mary of Częstochowa Church 120
St Mary's Basilica 66
SS Peter & Paul's Church 68
Schindler, Oskar 95
seasons 10
Sendzimir Steelworks Factory 113
shopping 24–6, 46–7, 137
    Kazimierz 85
    Nowa Huta 114
    Old town & Wawel 72–3
    Zakopane 123
skating 36
skiing 116
socialist realism 104, 112–13

sport & activities 34–6, 116, 122
Stare Miasto 60–77
swimming 36
symbols & abbreviations 6

T
Tatra Museum 120
Tatra National Park Museum 122
Tatras mountains 122
taxis 58
theatre 20, 33, 72, 113
tickets 33

time difference 50
tipping 29
toilets 131
Torture Museum 120
tourist information 135–6
tours 47, 104
trams 54–5, 108
Treasury & Armoury 70

W
walking 47, 112–13, 122
Wawel 60–77
Wawel Cathedral 69, 70
Wawel Dragon 68

Wawel Hill 69–70
Wawel Hill cave 68
weather 10, 48–9
winter sports 36, 116, 122
Wyspiański, Stanisław 20, 22, 66, 70–1, 83
Wyspiański Museum 70–1

Z
Zakopane 116–26
Zakopane Style Museum 120–2
Zalew nad Dłubia 113
zoo 99–100

SPOTTED YOUR NEXT CITY BREAK?

... then these CitySpots will have you in the know in no time, wherever you're heading.

Covering 100 cities worldwide, these vibrant pocket guides are packed with practical listings and imaginative suggestions, making sure you get the most out of your break, whatever your taste or budget.

Available from all good bookshops, your local Thomas Cook travel store or browse and buy online at www.thomascookpublishing.com

Editorial/project management: Lisa Plumridge
Copy editor: Paul Hines
Layout/DTP: Alison Rayner

The publishers would like to thank the following individuals
and organisations for supplying their copyright photographs
for this book: Giacomo Bassi, page 19; Krzysztof Gebarowski/
Fotolia.com, page 117; Pepe Rosso Restaurant, page 87; Restauracja
Wierzynek, page 75; Visit Poland, pages 25, 42–3, 59 & 67; Richard
Schofield, all others.

Send your thoughts to
books@thomascook.com

- Found a great bar, club, shop or must-see sight that we don't feature?
- Like to tip us off about any information that needs a little updating?
- Want to tell us what you love about this handy little guidebook and
  more importantly how we can make it even handier?

Then here's your chance to tell all! Send us ideas, discoveries and
recommendations today and then look out for your valuable input
in the next edition of this title.

Email the above address (stating the title) or write to:
CitySpots Series Editor, Thomas Cook Publishing, PO Box 227,
Coningsby Road, Peterborough PE3 8SB, UK.